How to Pick the Right Small Business Opportunity

KENNETH J. ALBERT

How to Pick the Right Small Business Opportunity

THE KEY TO SUCCESS IN YOUR OWN BUSINESS

McGRAW-HILL BOOK COMPANY

*New York   St. Louis   San Francisco   Auckland   Bogotá
Düsseldorf   Johannesburg   London   Madrid   Mexico
Montreal   New Delhi   Panama   Paris   São Paulo
Singapore   Sydney   Tokyo   Toronto*

Library of Congress Cataloging in Publication Data

Albert, Kenneth J, date.
How to pick the right small business opportunity.

Includes index.
1. Self-employed.   2. Small business.   I. Title.
HD8036.A42   658'.022   77-7780
ISBN 0-07-000947-3

1234567890   MUBP   786543210987

The editors for this book were Robert A. Rosenbaum and
Virginia Anne Fechtmann, the designer was Elliot Epstein,
and the production supervisor was Teresa F. Leaden.
It was set in Times Roman by Bi-Comp, Incorporated.

Printed by The Murray Printing Company and bound by
The Book Press.

To my wife Carol
To Kenny and Bruce
To my mother
And especially to my father—
he would have been proud

CONTENTS

PART III: SELECTING YOUR SPECIFIC OPPORTUNITY

PART IV: NOW YOU'RE READY TO BEGIN

PREFACE

You can start a successful business of your own—without taking any unnecessary risks and without a lot of capital. And you don't need any specialized knowledge or years of experience. By following the step-by-step approach spelled out in the chapters of this book, you can pick a business opportunity that will start you on your way to reaping the profits and rewards of having your own business.

PICKING THE RIGHT BUSINESS OPPORTUNITY IS THE KEY TO SUCCESS

Picking the right business opportunity means making sure, before starting out, that you choose a viable and profitable business—one that will meet your income expectations. And it means making a choice in a field that will grow and expand in the future. More specifically, it means making the right decision regarding such critical factors as location, product mix, gross margin, and so forth.

But most importantly, picking the right business means choosing an opportunity that suits your capabilities, and that provides an enjoyable, challenging, and fulfilling work environment. Then the work will seem like fun and will lead to success because:

> If you enjoy and find fulfillment in your work, you are much more likely to do an outstanding job. And if you do an outstanding job, you are much more likely to succeed.

SUCCESS MEANS MONEY AND MUCH MORE

More so than ever before, men and women are frustrated and unfulfilled in their jobs. They've had it with company politics, with rules and regulations, and with boring, repetitive work. The search for an alternative that offers independence and satisfaction has led many people to start businesses of their own.

These people are starting their own businesses not just for the money, but for all the things that owning a business can provide:

- Substantial income

- Personal achievement

- Status and recognition

- Enjoyable, meaningful work

- Pleasant, self-determined life-style

CHOOSING A BUSINESS IS ONE OF LIFE'S IMPORTANT DECISIONS

Selecting the right opportunity is the single most important decision associated with starting a successful small business. In fact, it quite likely will be the single most important decision in your entire business career.

Choosing the right business ranks in importance with selecting a marriage partner. In both cases, once the decision is made, you have to live with it. And there is another important similarity between picking a business and picking a spouse. The right choice leads to success in both situations. In business, as in marriage, once there is a good match, all the problems and difficulties that are encountered can be overcome through desire and hard work.

THERE IS A SUREFIRE WAY TO
PICK THE RIGHT BUSINESS

Starting a small business can involve many risks—risks that cause most to dismiss the idea as an impossible dream. Yet small business risks can be reduced to a tolerable level by systematically selecting the right small business opportunity—one that suits your wants and desires, one that fits your capabilities and limitations, and one that provides long-term profitability.

That brings us to the million-dollar question. Is there a way to select the right small business opportunity among the multitude of choices, in our complex and ever-changing economy? The answer is yes. And that's the reason for this book: to present a logical, straightforward, step-by-step approach that shows you how to select the right business opportunity for you.

HOW THE PROS SELECT SUCCESSFUL
BUSINESS OPPORTUNITIES AND
HOW YOU CAN DO IT TOO

Most people choose business opportunities the wrong way. They don't attempt to match their capabilities and desires with the business they select. And they don't properly investigate income potential and the strengths of competitors. Too often they rely on hot tips or on the recommendation of a friend or relative. More often than not, these poorly thought-out business ventures end in failure.

But this need not be the case. There is a sound way to choose your business, a logical and highly reliable approach used by the pros—large companies and management consultants—for years with a great deal of success. And the beauty of it is that you can use this proven approach to select a successful business of your own in your spare time. You don't have to be an expert. All you need to know is in this book. You'll see how to:

- Evaluate your capabilities and limitations

- Develop your business selection criteria

- Make your list of business types

- Select the right business opportunity by getting the facts:

    for franchises

    for ongoing businesses

    for start-up opportunities

- Check your selection to ensure success

And the last chapters of this book are devoted to getting you off on the right foot. Invaluable hints on getting started are presented, and you'll also find the basic keys to operating your business successfully.

The professional approach to business selection, which uses time-tested business research and analysis techniques, will demonstrate its worth to you. It will guide you toward selecting a healthy and vigorous business opportunity that offers substantial rewards today and growth for tomorrow.

I want to thank the management consulting firms that I've been associated with over the years for providing me with the opportunity to learn the techniques that are described in this book. And a special thanks to the many small business owners who have so generously shared with me their experiences and insights. Finally, a fond thank-you to Mrs. Ethel Vavruska for her help in typing this manuscript.

KEN ALBERT

Elmhurst, Illinois

How to Pick the Right Small Business Opportunity

1

INTRODUCTION

To be what we are, and to become what we are
capable of becoming, is the only end of life.
SPINOZA

Recently I had lunch with an old school friend who works for a large company in Chicago. He seemed in an unusually sullen mood. After ordering, he told me of a very important decision he had just made: "Ken, I've had it up to my ears with my job. I've got to find a way to be my own boss and do my own thing. There must be more to life than driving in to that place every day. I'm fed up with waiting for my boss to retire or die before I get a promotion."

I told Bill that I sympathized with him and that I admired his conviction and ambition. Then I asked him what type of business he was considering. "Well," he said, "I haven't really made up my mind. I've been kicking around the idea of going into manufacturing. But it seems so risky. Maybe I'd be better off with something safer like an Aamco or Midas franchise. I just don't know. But I do know that I'm going to do something. What do you think?"

I'm afraid I just confused the issue by asking Bill if he'd considered two other types of businesses that I thought might fit his background. You see, Bill is an avid Early American antiques collector. He also loves to travel and always makes detailed itineraries for each trip. "How about an antique shop or a travel agency?" I said.

Bill admitted he had never really considered those two possibilities but that they sounded interesting. In a few minutes we had a list of about ten more types of businesses that might be right for Bill. He looked at me and said, "How am I ever going to choose the right one for me? I could lose a bundle if I get into something that doesn't work out."

There is little doubt that Bill has the desire and skills to succeed in a business of his own—that is, if he doesn't select a loser or something he's not suited for. Perhaps you find yourself in the same predicament as Bill. Or maybe you have a slightly different problem; you know the type of business you want to start but you don't know which specific opportunity is best. For example, you know you want to buy a fast-food franchise, but of the dozens around, you don't know which one is the best bet. Well there are many people who are worried about the risks and are confused and bewildered by all the alternatives, but more than anything they want to have their own business—to be their own boss.

LUCK—DON'T COUNT ON IT

Choosing a business is one of the most important decisions of your life, yet most people do it by chance or coincidence. Some people are lucky and hit the right opportunity. I know of a business that was started by a fellow who was working as a chemical engineer for a large plastics company. He developed a new plastic compound that was a combination of a new material and a recycled material. When his employer decided to commercialize the new compound, they were unable to find a supplier of the recycled material. They had only expected to purchase about $200,000 worth of the material each year, and the big chemical suppliers weren't interested in such a "small" order. But our chemical engineer was in the right place at the right time. He seized the opportunity. Using a purchase order for $200,000, he secured the needed capital from a local bank, resigned his job, bought the necessary recycling equipment, and rented a small building. Five years later his business was grossing $4 million a year in sales. He then sold it to a large New York Stock Exchange–listed conglomerate for over $2 million. We should all have the luck and the foresight of this engineer.

But for every rags-to-riches story there are hundreds of failures—boarded-up storefronts, going-out-of-business sales, and broken dreams for people who started the wrong business, in the wrong neighborhood, at the wrong time. Many people start a business based on the recommendation of a relative or friend, or because they see what they presume to be a hot, new growth area. But decisions based on friendly recommendations or hunches are dangerous. Just because your brother-in-law owns a restaurant doesn't mean that you'll succeed in, or enjoy, the restaurant business. And just because quick-printing and furniture-refinishing shops are springing up all over doesn't mean they'll still be prospering two or three years from now. I know a man who bought an accounting service franchise ($10,000) based on a friend's recommendation. The franchising company went broke two months later, and the $10,000 was gone forever. And an acquaintance of mine secretly rushed into a home-sewing fabric business just before the home-sewing craze stagnated. He liquidated the business at a great financial loss after about a year of struggling in a saturated and highly competitive market. These are just two examples of mistakes that could have been avoided. Dun and Bradstreet estimates that about ten thousand businesses fail each year, and newly started businesses account for most of the casualties. Even starting an apparently "sure thing," like a soft-drink bottling franchise or an automobile dealership, could turn out to be a financial disaster if the opportunity is not analyzed properly beforehand.

THERE IS A BETTER WAY

There is a logical and systematic way to choose a business opportunity. If you're not sure about the type of business you want to start or are having trouble selecting the specific opportunity, I'm sure this approach can help you. It will greatly improve your chances of success. This step-by-step screening and selection process has been used by big corporations for years with a good deal of success. Of course big companies still make mistakes. The Edsel passenger car introduced by Ford Motor Company is probably one of the most famous. But compare that one mistake with Ford's list of successful new cars, including Thunderbird, Mustang, Maverick, Cougar, Mark IV, Pinto, Mustang II, Granada, and Monarch. I count nine successful new car introductions over the last twenty years. Nine winners out of ten, or 90 percent, is an excellent track record by anyone's standards.

You might be saying right now: "Sure that's fine for Ford. They probably have hundreds of people and spend millions of dollars each year on analyzing potential new products. I can't do anything like that, I'm only one person." You're right, but Ford is really one of the exceptions among big companies. Let me give you a sampling of down-to-earth business opportunities that some large companies have analyzed in the past several years:

- Analysis of a franchised restaurant chain
- Outlook for indoor tennis facilities
- Site selection for a restaurant in Philadelphia
- Opportunities in the office coffee service business
- Potential opportunities in houseplants
- Opportunities in the beauty shop business
- Analysis of the market for a new pet-care product
- Potential acquisition of a grandfather-clock manufacturer
- Analysis of the potential for door-to-door selling

All the above projects were carried out for major, well-known, U.S. corporations by hired consultants. Each was completed in less than three months, usually by one person. Average workdays of effort probably numbered about thirty days. The single most important point is that the consultants who carried out these projects didn't do anything you couldn't do with some time, effort, and desire. I've used the same business selection methods to analyze personal business opportunities such as mail order and commercial real estate brokerage. And a friend of mine thoroughly analyzed a franchised maternity shop opportunity before deciding to make a commitment.

YOU'VE GOT AN ADVANTAGE

And you know, you've got something extra going for you that a consultant or staff marketing analyst can't ever have. That's the personal enthusiasm that comes from knowing that you're evaluating a business opportunity for yourself, not for some large, cold, unfeeling corporation. This enthusiasm coupled with your feelings and instincts about yourself will probably result in your doing a better job. I know that it has worked out that way for me. I've analyzed hundreds of business opportunities for large companies, but I never really feel personally involved. It's just an assignment that I know will end in a couple of months and be filed away. But when I look at a business opportunity for myself, it's a whole different story. It's your future and your money that's on the line, so do that little bit extra.

IT'S A PERSONAL DECISION

Selecting a small business opportunity is really very personal. A business that may be perfectly suited to one person may be, and probably is, all wrong for most other people. Some businesses require an outgoing personality and an aggressive sales approach, while others depend on a good deal of patience and word-of-mouth advertising. Some businesses require a high degree of technical competence and others require none at all. And some businesses will require you to work every weekend while some others (like being a manufacturer's representative) probably will limit your primary business activity to weekdays from 9 A.M. to 5 P.M. Another personal consideration, which many people don't think of until it's too late, is the geographical mobility of a business. With most businesses, where you start them is where you have to keep them. But there are a few exceptions, such as mail order or direct marketing. I know a man who just recently moved his mail-order business from Chicago to Colorado Springs without losing a customer. In fact, this is one of the advantages that originally interested me enough to analyze the mail-order business. My analysis, however, uncovered some characteristics that convinced me that the mail-order business was not suited to me personally. (I'll tell you about these characteristics in one of the examples later on in the book.) The point I'm trying to make is that it's extremely important to select a business that satisfies your personal goals, that involves the kind of work you like to do and are good at, and that fits the life-style you want to have. When you find that "right business" you'll have the enthusiasm, energy, and stamina that it takes to succeed. And probably more important than financial success, at least to my way of thinking, you will be happy in your life's work.

THE TWO-STEP APPROACH

Two distinct steps are required in selecting a small business opportunity (see Figure 1). Step one is to select the type of business that best suits your personal goals, work requirements, and life-style desires. By type of business, I mean the answer you get when you ask someone the question "What business are you in?"—answers such as:

- We make small, engineered, plastic parts.

- I own a restaurant.

- I have an art gallery.

- I own a Midas Muffler shop.

- Oh, I'm a manufacturer's rep.

- I'm a real estate broker.

- I run a nursery.

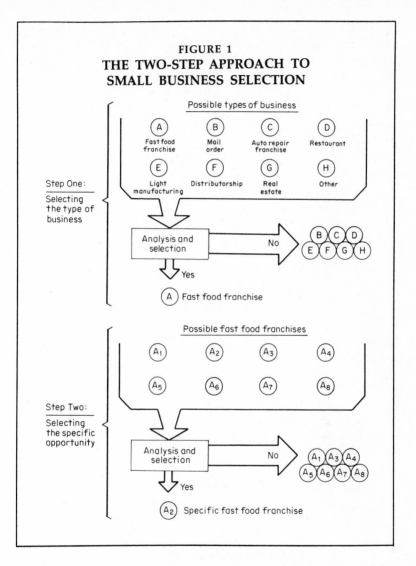

FIGURE 1
THE TWO-STEP APPROACH TO SMALL BUSINESS SELECTION

That's what I mean by type of business. And this step in the selection process really depends on what you want a business to bring to you.

The second step in the selection process is choosing the specific business opportunity, within the type of business classification you've selected in step one. For example, suppose you've gone through the "business type" screening and selection process of step one and decided that an antique shop is the type of business for you. Fine, you're off to a good start. But now you've got to select that specific right opportunity, and to do that you'll need answers to a lot of questions, important questions such as:

- Should you start your business from scratch or buy an ongoing concern?
- And if you decide to start from scratch:

  How do you select the best location?

  How many square feet of space do you need?

  How much money will be required for start-up expenses and inventory?

  What should you know about leases?

- Or if you buy an ongoing business:

  How successful has it been? Why?

  What future potential does it have?

  Why is it really for sale?

  Is the success of the business dependent upon the personal talents and contacts of the present owner?

  How much is the business really worth?

- And once you're in business:

  What is the best way to buy merchandise?

  Which products sell best? Why?

  What gross margins should you aim for?

  What are the most effective advertising and promotion methods?

In what season should you expect peaks and lulls?

What about fire and theft insurance?

And what are your Social Security and tax obligations?

Getting answers to these types of questions, and analyzing and interpreting them properly, is the most important part of selecting a specific business opportunity. This book will show you how you can do it.

MY BACKGROUND

I think you should know a little bit about me. I have extensive experience in screening and analyzing business and new-product opportunities for small and large companies—and for myself. Most of my professional experience has been as a management consultant for a large marketing consulting firm. And the screening and analysis that I've done for myself has been done mostly in my spare time. Actually, I'm a product of the somewhat misdirected emphasis that was placed on higher education during the fifties and sixties. I came from a very modest, yet loving, homelife, so I decided that engineering would give me the success and security I thought I wanted. After graduation, I went to work for a large aerospace firm. And after that I began advancing "by degrees" so to speak. First, I got a master's in engineering, which qualified me for a lower-level engineering management position with a large, heavy-equipment manufacturer. Then I went back to school again and got a master's degree in business administration. That landed me my first job in the management consulting business.

But like so many other people, I've never really been happy being an employee. I've worked for large companies, small companies, manufacturing companies, professional service organizations, and I've made a comfortable living. Yet I've always had a gnawing feeling that I would be happier if I were self-employed.

As time passed I became more and more frustrated and unhappy with the "company mentality." So I started employing the business analysis and selection techniques I'd been using as a management consultant to select a self-employment opportunity for myself. And, in fact, I found an opportunity that is perfectly suited to my wants and desires using the techniques I describe in this book.

YOU WON'T BE ALONE

You know, sometimes, it seems that the small business owner in this country is almost a dying breed. I know that most of my relatives, friends, and acquaintances work for this or that company or institution. It seems that most everybody is an employee. But closer examination of the facts indicates that there are a great number of small business owners and self-employed people in this country. Just look at these statistics:

- 2,400,000 retailers with sales less than $1 million per year
- 420,000 small wholesalers
- 400,000 franchised small businesses
- 390,000 manufacturers with sales of less than $1 million per year

Or start to think of all the small business owners in your community or neighborhood. They really add up when you count all the retailers, franchises, and small distributing and manufacturing companies. What this all says to me is that even though you'll be joining a minority when you start your own business, it is a strong and healthy minority. And most of your "employed" friends will be a little jealous and maybe even wish that they could muster the nerve to follow your example.

ORGANIZATION

This book is organized into four sections. The first section focuses on the importance of the individual in selecting a small business opportunity. By examining your likes and dislikes, and your strengths and weaknesses, we can determine what you expect to receive from a specific business ,and the capabilities that you bring to it. And then I'll show you how motivation can be used to conquer shortcomings such as a lack of experience.

The second section is devoted to showing you how to use the information developed in section one to select the type of business that fits you best. The business analysis and selection techniques that you will need are described in detail.

In the third section we really get down to the nitty-gritty— selecting a specific business opportunity. I'll show you how the large companies do it and how you can do it too, for a franchise, for an ongoing business, and for a start-from-scratch opportunity.

If you are absolutely sure, right now, about the type of business you want to start, you might be tempted to skip right to section three and get going on selecting your specific opportunity. I wouldn't do that if I were you—for two reasons. First, you'll miss some of the business analysis techniques you'll need to make your selection. Second, by going through the self-analysis and business type selection process you might be surprised to discover a type of business, one you never even thought of before, that you like better than your initial choice.

The fourth, and final, section of the book focuses on some helpful hints and advice to get you off to a good start. Time-tested principles of success are discussed as well as the important contribution that your spouse can make.

The whole process of analyzing, selecting, and starting a business of your own probably sounds overwhelming by now. But it really isn't. Hundreds of thousands of people from all backgrounds and all walks of life have started successful small businesses. You can do it too. All you need is the desire to succeed and the patience to take it one step at a time.

PART

I

YOU'RE THE KEY

2

WHAT DO YOU WANT FROM A BUSINESS OF YOUR OWN?

It is not enough to be busy; so are the ants.
The question is: What are we busy about?
HENRY DAVID THOREAU

Yes, I know you want what everybody else wants from their own business—such things as independence, wealth, and status. But which is most important, and aren't you also seeking personal satisfaction, an opportunity to be creative, or a chance to make a lasting contribution to society? Maybe you are and maybe you aren't, but surely you're interested in doing the type of work that you'll enjoy and in interacting with customers in a way that will make you feel most comfortable and relaxed. And what about the impact of your own business on the personal life you want for yourself and your family? Independence and financial security aren't much good if your business prevents you from enjoying the fruits of your labors.

So you see, there are many things that you should consider before you decide what you really want from a business. The decision is fairly complicated because of the potential conflicts between specific rewards you might be seeking. For example, a desire for a high degree of personal creativity may be inconsistent with a desire for great monetary wealth. Or a desire to express an interest in gourmet cooking by operating a small, intimate French restaurant may conflict with the desire to spend evenings and weekends with the family. We're going to sort out all these issues in this chapter and get them organized, because once you have clearly stated what you want from a business, this statement becomes your business selection criteria.

It's the same kind of thing you would do if you were going to buy a house. You'd have to define what you want in a house— number of bedrooms, distance from transportation and shopping, Cape Cod or ranch style, and so on. This definition then becomes your house selection criteria. The same thing is true for a business, only it's much more complicated and, in most cases, more important to your future well-being and happiness.

BUSINESS SELECTION CRITERIA

The business selection criteria is made up of nine elements that deal with financial and personal goals, business work requirements, and the impact of a small business on the owner's lifestyle. In this chapter, each of these elements is discussed, and important considerations, guidelines, and examples are pointed out. Figure 2 is a guide to help you develop your own selection criteria. I think you will find it very helpful in clearly stating, on one piece of paper, your personal business selection preferences. After reading the section on each element, decide on your own preference and fill in the appropriate portion of the guide.

Your business selection criteria (to repeat, what you want from a business of your own) will be used later on to screen a large group of different types of businesses. In this way you'll be able to select the type of business that comes closest to meeting your criteria. So you see, it's very important that we determine, and clearly state, what we want from a business. For simplicity, the discussion that will help you in defining your criteria is divided into three major sections: (1) goals, (2) the work, and (3) life-style impact.

Goals

Your Annual Income.   How much do you want to earn each year after your business is running smoothly? How about $20,000,

FIGURE 2
BUSINESS SELECTION CRITERIA GUIDE

Goals

- **Your Annual Income** □ $10–20,000   □ $40–60,000   □ $80–100,000
  (check one)   □ $20–40,000   □ $60–80,000   □ Over $100,000

- **Personal Achievement** (1)_____
  (fill-in)
                       (2)_____

                       (3)_____

- **Importance of Status**   □ Important   □ Moderately   □ Not
  (check one)   important   important

The Work

- **Content**   □ With hands   □ Alone   □ Manufacturing
  (check   □ Paper work   □ With   □ Management
  preferences)   □ Outdoors   people   □ Sales

- **People Contact**   □ Suppliers   □ Retail sales
  (check preferences)   □ Employees   □ Personal selling

- **How Much**   □ Permanent full time
  (choose one)   □ Eventual (5–10 years) part time
                     □ Eventual absentee ownership

Life-Style

- **Business Hours**   □ M–F, 9–5   □ Saturdays
  (check acceptable)   □ Evenings   □ Sundays

- **Other Business Impact** □ Overnight   Proximity to home_____
  (check all acceptable   travel   miles
  and fill in)   □ Entertain   Preferred city
                            customers   Now_____
                            □ Emergency   Future_____
                            calls

$50,000, $100,000, or more. It's important to decide on an income goal, because different types of businesses have different income potentials. A fast-food restaurant has one income potential and a small manufacturing business may have quite another.

It's probably tempting to set your goal at a very high level—say even a million dollars a year. And in principle that's fine. Many businesses have the long-run potential of making their founders into millionaires. A small restaurant can become a large restaurant, which could eventually become a franchised chain of restaurants. But then again, many other businesses will never become million-dollar operations. Most single-location franchise opportunities fall into this category. The average McDonald's Hamburgers restaurant has annual gross sales of about $600,000. Income, after expenses (payroll, food and supplies, rent, etc.) in most cases is probably significantly less than $100,000. Which is still a very good figure, but it's not now, nor will it ever be, anywhere near a million dollars per year.

I know a bright young man, a Harvard Business School graduate, who wants to become a millionaire. In fact, he wants it so much that it really is the singular goal of his life. However, because of this goal, he rejects almost all the business opportunities that he is exposed to, because "they're not million-dollar potentials." Try to set your goal realistically so this doesn't happen to you. There are many fine businesses that bring a lifetime of satisfaction to their owners without earning a million dollars.

Well, enough preaching on the potential dangers of overstating your income goal. I've found that the easiest way for a person to set his or her personal income goal is to answer the question "How much do I want to be making per year five years from now?" Give it some thought and then decide on your answer. Indicate your income goal by checking the appropriate box at the top of the business selection guide in Figure 2.

Personal Achievement.   Now that we've established your income goal, let's move on to a type of goal that is quite different. It's called personal achievement, and it's really nothing more or nothing less than what you, as an individual, want it to be. The most obvious personal achievement goal is to build a successful business, which is quite an achievement in itself. But if you begin to think about it, you may have additional personal goals. Probably the best way to show you what I mean is with some examples of goals that people have expressed to me:

- To provide work opportunities for minorities and the handicapped
- To build a business that will provide for my family after I'm gone
- To contribute something worthwhile and lasting to society
- To do something that will give me a small piece of immortality
- To maximize my percentage of enjoyable time each day
- To travel and see the world
- To express my personal artistic creativity
- To gain some form of positive recognition
- To fulfill my purpose for being on earth
- To help underprivileged teen-age boys

This list is obviously not complete. It's only intended to start you thinking. You might want to mull it over for a while and then come back to it. When you've defined the personal achievement goals that relate to your business, fill them in on Figure 2.

Importance of Status.   We all know what status is and most of us profess not to be interested in it. Yet we're all concerned with what other people think of us. "They" influence our choice of clothing, the car we drive, the neighborhood we live in, and even where and when and how often we go on vacation. I'm afraid that all of us are status seekers and name-droppers to at least a modest degree. And some of us seem to thrive on it.

Businesses have their status too, there are high-status businesses and low-status businesses. Junk collecting is an obvious low-status business, and being a Cadillac dealer is an obvious high-status business. But there are more subtle differences. There is a different status in owning a Burger King franchise and owning a Victoria Station franchise even though both are restaurants. And it's true in manufacturing also. A manufacturer of surgical instruments has a higher status than a manufacturer of nuts and bolts.

Some people are very interested in the status of their business and others are not interested at all. I'm not siding with either group. I'm just suggesting that it may be an important consideration in selecting the type of business for you. The key is to choose a business that has a status that you'll feel comfortable with. When you've decided how you feel about status, indicate your choice on Figure 2.

The Work

Content. It's true that in most small businesses you've got to do a little bit of everything—from selling, to bookkeeping, to production, to cleaning up. But it's also true that a specific type of work dominates, or takes up the bulk of the owner's waking hours, in most small businesses. That's the work content that we're focusing on. For example, in a small metal fabricating operation, you'd either be spending most of your time in production or in sales. I know of a business of this type that was started by two brothers. In the early days of the business they rotated. The first week one operated the production equipment and the other one called on customers. The next week they switched. Eventually the older brother settled into production permanently, and the younger one devoted all his time to selling. (Incidentally, this business, which is now about twenty years old, had sales of $18 million last year!) A very different situation exists in a small bookkeeping service company. The owner of this type of company will spend much of his time alone, working on clients' books.

The key to defining your work-content business selection criteria is to isolate the types of work you enjoy most. Do you enjoy making things with your hands? Do you enjoy paper work? Do you enjoy personal persuasion and selling? Do you have a strong preference for working indoors, or outdoors? Review your background to select the work experiences you've enjoyed most. And don't limit your thinking only to your workday experience. Try to choose the work you enjoyed most in all your experiences and activities. Things such as hobbies, civic activities, and schooling should be included in your search for the work content you prefer. Note all the tasks you've enjoyed over the years, and you'll soon begin to see a pattern emerge. One, two, or even three types of work activities will stand out as being your favorites. Fill these in on the business selection criteria guide.

People Contact.   How do you feel about working with other people? Do you really enjoy it, or do you wish you could always work alone, or are you somewhere in between? Well, your interaction with other people is the subject of this selection criteria. People contact is really a part of work content, the section we just finished, but people relations are such an important topic that I decided to devote a separate section to them.

There are really three types of people contact in a small business: contact with customers, employees, and suppliers. Most small business owners don't mind the contact with employees and suppliers, since the owner is usually on the most comfortable side of the relationship. Being the boss or being the buyer is always more comfortable than being the employee or being the seller. But in the third form of contact, with the customer, the small business owner is on the other side of the fence—the uncomfortable side. And the owner-customer relationship differs greatly depending on the type of business you're in. For example, in real estate brokerage, personal aggressive selling is the name of the game, and it could include entertaining clients and their spouses, golf outings on Saturday morning, and so on. If you don't enjoy personal selling, don't choose a business where it's required. Many businesses have a much more impersonal sales approach. In most retail operations, for example, successful selling depends more on good merchandise, fair prices, and advertising than it does on handshakes and smiles. An extreme example of impersonal selling is mail order, where you never even see a customer (customers send in orders and the owner sends out the merchandise). Give some thought to the people contact you like in a work situation and then note it on Figure 2.

How Much. Starting a small business takes a lot of hard work. In fact, it may consume most of your waking hours in the first few years. But in the longer run, work effort and personal involvement on the part of a small business owner can vary a great deal. In many established small businesses, many day-in-and-day-out activities can be turned over to a manager. I know of a small machine shop where the owner works only two or three days per week. However, absentee ownership, even on a partial basis, is not possible in some small businesses. For example, in many franchise operations, sales are not large enough to support an owner's profits and a manager's salary. And in other businesses, the owner's contribution is so intimately involved with the success of the business that it's impossible for the owner to be away from the business for more than a few days at a time.

Decide on the personal involvement and work effort you'd like to put into your business five to ten years from now. Quite conceivably, you'll want to continue to be fully involved. Or maybe you'll prefer to ease up a little. Note your work involvement business selection criteria on Figure 2.

Life-Style

Business Hours. As a 9 to 5, Monday to Friday employee you might not have given much thought to the hours that many small businesses are open. But with a little observation, it becomes obvious, very quickly, that many small businesses don't operate on a Monday through Friday, 9 to 5 schedule. Take my recent experience as a consumer, for example. Just in the last couple weeks, my wife and I went out to dinner on a Saturday night, we stopped at a convenience grocery store at 10:30 P.M. on Tuesday evening, and last weekend we found ourselves browsing around in a little antique shop at 3:30 on a Saturday afternoon. And if I think back several years, the real estate agent showed us the home we're now living in on a Sunday afternoon. None of these small businesses (restaurant, convenience store, antique shop, real estate) operated on a 9 to 5 schedule.

If you enjoy a normal workweek, and don't want to give it up when you start your business, you've got to be careful when you choose your business. Of course, even if you choose manufacturing or wholesaling or some other normal workweek business, there will be much work to do beyond regular business hours. But a good deal of freedom exists in scheduling, during nonbusiness hours, things such as bookkeeping, dictating, et cetera. Have you decided on your business hours selection criteria? If so, fill it in on Figure 2.

Other Business Impact. We've just seen how business hours can have a major impact on your life-style. But there are many more subtle ways a business can affect your life-style. For example, being a manufacturer's representative may require heavy out-of-town travel, which means nights and evenings away from the family. Personal selling businesses may also require you to entertain customers on evenings or weekends. Another area of major impact is the location of a specific business. Many businesses, to be successful, must be near a large concentration of potential customers. To effectively manage a business, and to keep commuting time within reason, most small business owners live near their businesses. So if you buy or start a small business thirty miles or more from your present home, you may eventually decide to move your family. Speaking of moving, it can't be done with most businesses, especially consumer product or service operations. So, for example, if you start a business in Minneapolis, you're going to have to live with the cold winters as long as you have the business.

A final example of the impact a business can have on the owner's life-style is emergency calls and customer complaints. There's that old joke about the doctor who, when his hot-water heater sprung a leak in the middle of the night, calls a plumber. The plumber vengefully answers the doctor's call for help with, "Give it two aspirins and call me in the morning." Unfortunately, if you're operating a plumbing or heating business, calls in the middle of the night and on Sundays will be no joke. And customers have a way of "calling the owner at home" to complain about poor service or a faulty product. You've maybe even done that once or twice yourself. Mull some of these examples over in your mind and then fill in, on the guide, your sensitivity to other business impacts on your future life-style.

YOUR OWN CRITERIA

Well, you just finished developing your own small business selection criteria. How does it look to you? It is hoped that you now have a much better understanding of what you want from a small business. What does your business selection criteria mean? We'll get to that later when we compare your criteria with numerous types of small business alternatives. But first, in the next chapter, we're going to examine the capabilities, strengths, and weaknesses you bring to a small business opportunity.

3

ASSESSING THE CAPABILITIES YOU BRING TO A BUSINESS

*The most difficult thing in
life is to know yourself.*
THALES

In the last chapter, we looked at what you want from a business of your own. In this chapter, we will examine and categorize the capabilities you can bring to a business opportunity. Self-examination is always difficult, primarily because it's not easy to be honest with oneself. But honesty is really the key to meaningful self-examination, so do try to be as honest with yourself as you can while assessing your capabilities.

Some health experts suggest that the best way to tell if you are even slightly overweight is to take off all your clothes and look at yourself in a full-length mirror. It sounds like a very effective method of self-examination. Maybe we can apply it to our situation. No, I'm not suggesting you examine your capabilities while sitting in the nude. But all of us do carry around a protective layer to insulate our ego from continual bombardment. It might be well to strip this away in our quest for an honest self-assessment.

Defining the capabilities you can bring to a business is extremely important. In the second section of this book, you'll see how the information developed in this chapter, along with the business selection criteria developed in the last chapter, will be used to select the type of business that best suits you. Assessing your capabilities is really quite simple. It only requires a self-examination in five categories. So that your assessment will be in a usable format when we get into actual business selection, it's probably best to use the capability assessment guide in Figure 3. On this guide the five categories are listed with space provided for your responses.

In the remaining sections of this chapter, each category area on the guide is discussed in detail. There are questions to ask your-

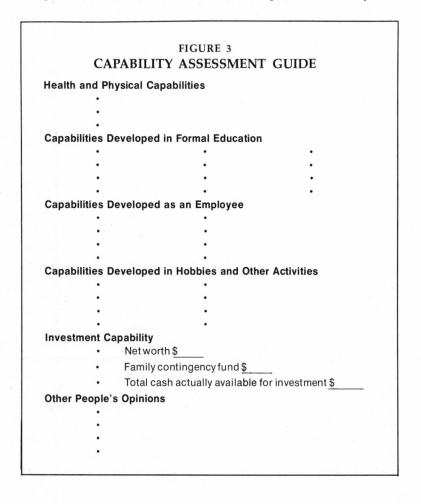

FIGURE 3
CAPABILITY ASSESSMENT GUIDE

Health and Physical Capabilities
- •
- •
- •

Capabilities Developed in Formal Education
- •   •   •
- •   •   •
- •   •   •

Capabilities Developed as an Employee
- •   •
- •   •
- •   •
- •   •

Capabilities Developed in Hobbies and Other Activities
- •   •
- •   •
- •   •
- •   •

Investment Capability
- •   Net worth $____
- •   Family contingency fund $____
- •   Total cash actually available for investment $____

Other People's Opinions
- •
- •
- •
- •

self in each category, as well as important considerations and guidelines, and examples are presented to stimulate your thinking. Read each section and give your response some thought before writing it down. You'll probably find some of the questions and considerations in each category very easy. Others may require a good deal of thought and probing. Don't be discouraged if it takes you several hours, or days, to complete the guide. It has been designed to encourage you to probe deeply into your experiences and background.

There remains one additional consideration before moving on to the categories themselves. If your spouse or a partner is likely to be involved in your business, it would be wise for them also to fill in the capability assessment guide. In this way you might find some complimentary skills that will strengthen your potential for success. On the other hand, you might also uncover some common weakness that will suggest avoiding certain types of business opportunities.

HEALTH AND PHYSICAL CAPABILITIES

Do you have any health limitations or physical considerations which will limit the type of business activities you can engage in? This is the primary question to answer in this category. It may be that you're older or have a circulation problem that prevents you from standing for long periods of time. Such a condition might prevent you from functioning effectively in many retail business opportunities such as restaurants, boutiques, beauty shops, and so forth. Some businesses require a good deal of driving. So if a back condition or some other limitation precludes extensive driving, note this on the capability assessment guide. A somewhat more obscure situation where a bad back could limit your effectiveness is in a Rent-All operation. Lifting a heavy Rototiller into the trunk of a customer's car could put you in traction and close your business.

Of course, some physical conditions could limit your activities in almost any business you choose. For example, arthritis or poor vision could prevent you from typing invoices or making entries on your books. But don't be too concerned about these types of problems. There are companies that are in the business of providing recordkeeping, stenographic, and other services to small businesses. Give your health limitations and physical considerations some serious thought and briefly note your conclusions on the guide. It's also probably a good idea to try to anticipate five and ten years into the future. Obviously, you can't foresee most illnesses or injuries, but by taking your age and current physical condition into account, you may be able to make at least a rough estimate of your future physical condition. But if you're 50 or 55 now, or even 65, don't let it deter you from starting your own business. If your general health is satisfactory you can still do it. After all, Ray Kroc started McDonald's Hamburgers at 49. And Colonel Sanders' Kentucky Fried Chicken restaurants were started when its founder was 65 years old.

CAPABILITIES DEVELOPED IN FORMAL EDUCATION

Obviously, an extensive formal education is not an essential prerequisite for success in a small business. There are hundreds of stories of high school dropouts who have gone on to become extremely happy and successful entrepreneurs. And in fact, a formal education is probably of less importance in one's own business than it is as an employee in someone else's business. This is true because of the way companies go about hiring and promoting their employees. We all know that most companies exclude employment candidates and limit employee advancement because of "inadequate" education. This can't happen in your own business. Your success and growth is dependent only upon your capabilities and motivation.

What we're looking for in this section is not how much formal education you have, but what you got out of it. That is, what portions of your formal education could be helpful in your own business? Review your education experience for meaningful courses. Maybe you studied typing, shorthand, or bookkeeping in high school. Foreign languages could be very valuable in many businesses. Obviously, if you're contemplating a manufacturing business, technical courses (e.g., shops, sciences, engineering) will be helpful. If it's been a while since you've been in school, it might be helpful to "reconstruct" the courses you took each year on a sheet of paper. Then you can choose the relevant courses and transfer them to the guide in Figure 3.

CAPABILITIES DEVELOPED AS AN EMPLOYEE

What portions of your employment experience could be helpful in your own business? Obviously, the applicability of your employment experience to a small business will depend greatly on the particular type of work you've done and probably also on the size of the companies you've worked for. For example, often the least applicable work experience relates to people who've had very specialized jobs with very large companies. This was the case with my own work experience as a mechanical engineer during my first six years after college. For the first three years I did heat-transfer and fluid-flow design work on advanced aircraft jet engines. And in the next three years I was a development project engineer for a diesel-engine manufacturer. I guarantee that it's not easy to find relevant small business capability development from these work experiences. But I did get some value from it. I learned to work with, understand, and get along with people and computors. I learned how real-life business problems are solved. And probably most important, I learned that being an engineer for a large company was not going to be my life's work. My point is that no matter how obscure and esoteric your work experience is, it is of some value in a small business.

Almost all businesses have four basic functional areas:

1. Management

2. Finance and accounting

3. Design and production

4. Sales and marketing

Experience in any of these areas is extremely valuable in most small businesses. Review each of the jobs you've held and relate the relevant experience in each functional area. Admittedly, some work experience is hard to relate to these functions. For example, say your work experience has been concentrated as a machine mechanic in a large automotive plant. Is this relevant experience? Sure. You've had a great deal of exposure to production processes, you've developed your mechanical or electrical skills, and you've been relating on a daily basis to the single common denominator of business—people. Exposure in working with other people is always valuable. Or take a person who has been an executive secretary for the last five years. This exposure is obviously very relevant to starting a stenographic or part-time clerical-help business. And if your boss was, for example, controller of the company, surely the exposure to financial and accounting procedures is applicable to any small business. So you see, most work exposure is valuable in one way or another. Summarize the capabilities you developed in your employment experience by filling in the appropriate space in Figure 3.

BACKGROUND, HOBBIES, AND ACTIVITIES

Have you developed any skills or capabilities in your hobbies or other nonwork activities that could be applicable to a small business? I've found that the best way to approach this catchall category is to start with a list of all the things you're involved in. A typical list might include fishing, golf, PTA, political organizations, church activities, stamp collecting, gardening, photography, and astrology. The possibilities are endless. And don't overlook a category I call "nonwork" work activities. Some examples are professional organizations, union activities, bowling leagues, organizing company picnics, and so on. You may have had a good chance to develop your organizing and managerial skills in these areas.

Now that you've got your list, it's time to examine it in search of your capabilities. Take a friend of mine who's an avid stamp collector, for example. He prides himself on being a very adroit bidder at stamp auctions. This competitive "purchasing skill" could be a very valuable asset in any small business where "smart buying" leads to a competitive edge. Being president of your local PTA could be equally valuable in developing organizational and leadership skills.

One other area to screen for capabilities is your overall background. Look for character traits or work habits that you've developed over the years. Are you practical, pragmatic, or conscientious? Have others commented that you're a "hard worker" or have good common sense? These are extremely valuable capabilities and they should be noted along with the results from the search of your list of activities. Summarize your list on Figure 3.

INVESTMENT CAPABILITY

I'm sure it's no news to you that starting or buying a business takes money. And the amount of money required can vary a great deal. A few businesses can be started for as little as $1000 to $2000, while others require $100,000 or more. Most are probably in the $10,000 to $50,000 range. So it is important that we define what size investment you are capable of making. The simplest and most direct way to assess this capability is to calculate your net worth. A self-explanatory table is included in Figure 4 to assist you in your computations. Fill in all the applicable spaces and then go through the necessary additions and subtractions. Incidentally, a net-worth calculation is an integral part of almost all franchise applications. So if you're possibly interested in a franchised business opportunity, you'll be one step ahead by making your calculation now.

Well, how does it look? No doubt your net worth is not as large as you'd like. What's more, you probably can't invest all your net worth in a new business. First, there's the problem of fixed assets not being available for investment. Your house is probably the prime example. And second, you need a family contingency fund. Most family financial counselors recommend one year's net income. You could probably get away with a somewhat smaller amount if your spouse is working.

FIGURE 4
NET-WORTH CALCULATION TABLE

Assets		**Liabilities**	
Cash on hand and in bank	$ ____	Notes payable to bank	$ ____
Government securities	$ ____	Notes payable to others	$ ____
Stocks and/or bonds	$ ____	Accounts and bills due	$ ____
Accounts and notes receivable	$ ____	Real estate mortgage	
Real estate owned		Home	$ ____
Home	$ ____	Other	$ ____
Other	$ ____	Other debts	$ ____
Automobile	$ ____		$ ____
Cash surrender value—			$ ____
life insurance	$ ____		$ ____
Other Assets	$ ____	Total liabilities	$ ____
Total assets	$ ____		

Net-worth calculation:

Total assets	$ ____
Total liabilities	$ ____
Net worth (Total assets less liabilities)	$ ____

There are several steps you can take to improve your investment capabilities. Obviously, the first is to set up or expand a
formal savings plan. By eliminating some of your discretionary
purchases you may be able to save 10 percent or more of your net
income. Another readily available source of investment capital is
whole life insurance policies. You can borrow against their cash
value at a surprisingly low interest rate. On the capability assessment guide in Figure 3, space has been provided for relevant
investment capability information.

OTHER PEOPLE'S OPINIONS

There is one other very effective way to assess your capabilities. This chapter has focused, so far, on self-examination, but the opinions of people you respect can also be quite valuable. Often they see things (good or bad) that you have underestimated the importance of, or totally overlooked.

Before soliciting other people's opinions, review whatever opinions you may have collected in the past. Some colleges conduct faculty evaluation programs for graduating students. Dig yours out if you've got one and look it over. If you've worked for large companies, you've probably experienced the annual performance review. I know they've got their shortcomings, but you might be able to learn something from them. Try to look for patterns and consistent findings from year to year.

A specific list of questions will be helpful in soliciting other people's opinions. You can develop these from your own appraisal and from the opinions you've received in the past. Try to direct the questions at strengths and weaknesses that are still unclear in your mind. Here are some suggested questions to start you thinking.

- What do you think of my ability to judge other people?

- How do you rate my managerial skills?

- Do you think I lose my temper too often?

- How does my sales capability stack up?

When you've got your questions finished, you're ready to begin soliciting opinions. I'd suggest the following approach. Tell each person that you've always respected their ability to judge people (even if it's a little white lie). Go on to say that you'd appreciate it very much if he or she would answer a few personal questions for you. Ask the person to give perfectly honest responses. You can explain the real reason you're asking or just say it's "a personal improvement technique you saw in the

Reader's Digest." Ask your list of questions and follow the good answers with comments like "Could you expand on that"? or "That's interesting, what made you think of that?" These comments will encourage the person to be more honest and frank. Here are two questions to tack on the end of your list.

• What do you think my major strengths are? Why?

• What about my three major shortcomings?

The last step in this process is to review all the opinions you've collected and try to make some sense out of them. It is hoped that you will have found it to be an interesting and enlightening experience. Fill in a summary of your findings on the guide in Figure 3.

YOU MADE IT!

How does your capability assessment guide look now that you've got it completed? Don't be discouraged if it doesn't describe an impressive array of capabilities. Not very many of them do. Yours is probably very typical.

Well, we've just been through two chapters of filling in criteria guides, and tables. I feel a little bit apologetic about subjecting you to such a barrage. But it was necessary. And now that we've got your business selection criteria and your small business capabilities concisely stated, we're almost ready to begin the business selection process.

4

MOTIVATION IS THE
KEY INGREDIENT

*The three great essentials to achieve anything worthwhile are,
first, hard work; second, stick-to-itiveness; third, common sense.*

THOMAS ALVA EDISON

In the last two chapters we've developed a list of the things you
want from a business of your own (business selection criteria)
and a list of your capabilities. Comparing these two lists is dis-
couraging for most people mainly because on paper the "wants"
seem to require much more that the "capabilities" can ever hope
to deliver. But take heart, there is one capability that we haven't
discussed yet. And in many business situations, it's this intangible capability I call motivation that can make the difference. The
problem with this capability is that it is almost impossible to
know how much anyone has, that is, until a situation arises that
demands a great deal of motivation and stick-to-itiveness. That's
when the people with a determined spirit rise to the occasion.

Motivation is more than just another capability. It is the single
capability that can, and will, help you overcome a lack of
capabilities in other areas. In fact, motivation is the key ingredient to small business success. There are hundreds of examples
of people overcoming obstacles to achieve independence and
self-satisfaction in a business of their own. In particular, there is
one that always stands out in my mind. I'd like to share it with
you because it illustrates so well what motivation and desire can
accomplish.

Jim McGill was born and raised in a small town in Alabama. When he was 35, he and his wife inherited a smallish amount of cedar timberland. Jim had always dreamed of having his own business and he saw this cedar acreage as a way of getting started. Jim's business plan was to sell whatever he could that related to cedar. Since he had some sawmill experience, he began by mortgaging the land to purchase used sawmill and wood-finishing equipment. Initially he sold cedar logs and cedar lumber. Eventually he expanded into tongue-and-groove cedar boards for closet linings. About five years after starting his business, he began a successful line of cedar-chest kits that were sold through the mail.

By 1965, twenty years after he began, Jim was a long-established, modestly successful businessman. His annual sales were about $350,000. But Jim wasn't content, because he was never really able to find the one great product that would put him in the "big time." Over the years, the tongue-and-groove cedar-closet lining product never sold that well. Jim always felt that the product was limited by its high price and the necessity of installing thirty or forty individual boards in order to line a closet. In his spare time he had been toying with a system that used cedar chips and pressed them into a ¼-in. thick sheet. Eventually, he hoped to be able to produce relatively inexpensive 4 × 8 foot sheets of closet lining material. He envisioned a do-it-yourselfer buying three sheets at the local lumberyard and lining a closet by just cutting them to size. He was sure they would sell because even someone who was all thumbs could "build" a cedar closet in an afternoon for less than $20.

In the summer of 1965, Jim's cedar-sheet closet lining system was perfected to the point where he decided to order production equipment and a new plant to house it. The total cost was approximately $400,000. His timber holdings and other assets were used to secure the necessary loan.

Several months later disaster struck. Jim developed a sore on his arm that would not heal. His doctor diagnosed it as a rapidly spreading and almost always fatal form of skin cancer. Four months later Jim was dead. He had written his will on his deathbed. When Jim learned of his terminal illness, he tried to cancel the contract for the new plant, but it couldn't be done. He tried to sell the contract, but no one would buy it. To make matters worse, Jim had never elected to incorporate his business. Since he operated as a sole proprietorship, the high debt associated with the new plant not only threatened to destroy the business, but it also threatened everything the family owned, including the family home and all its furnishings.

In an effort to protect their security, Jim's family elected to continue operating the business. The responsibility for its management was assumed by Jim's second eldest child, Elaine. At the time she was 24 years of age and had never had any active involvement in the business. As a matter of fact, she had no business education or background whatsoever. But time was to show that she had the one thing she needed. She had the desire and the motivation to see it through. She had the will to succeed.

Elaine's difficulties seemed almost insurmountable. She not only had to learn the everyday operation of the ongoing business, but she also had to coordinate and supervise construction and start-up of the new cedar-closet lining plant. And, of course, by being so intimately involved with her father's business, she was constantly reminded of the great personal loss she and her family had suffered.

Elaine and her husband decided very early on that the business was strictly a family matter. Elaine and the family were going to sink or swim on their own. Therefore, Elaine's husband would not become actively involved in the business or participate in any of the decisions. His role was confined to giving Elaine huge doses of moral support.

It was about a year after Elaine took over the business that I first met her. One afternoon the president of the consulting firm I was with at the time called me into his office. It seems that a friend of Elaine's, who was also a friend of our firm, had suggested to her that "this consulting firm in Chicago" might be able to give her some assistance in the marketing area. Although as a rule we did not work for small companies, our president decided to accept the assignment as a personal favor.

The next morning at 9 A.M., the president of our firm and myself were pulling into the gravel parking lot of Elaine's inherited business. Neither of us knew quite what to expect. But we soon found out. There was Elaine, sitting behind a big desk in what was once her father's office. She was an extremely attractive and gracious Southern lady. Yet it became apparent very quickly that she was also very businesslike. And it seemed, at least outwardly, that she was confident and in absolute control. She explained that the cedar-closet lining plant was about to come on-stream and that she was seeking advice on distributing and marketing the 4 × 8 sheets of cedar. Both of us were amazed at how much she had learned and accomplished in just one year. After all, just twelve months before she was inexperienced, struggling to run a business she knew nothing about.

The next month we presented to Elaine a marketing plan for her new closet lining product. She did a beautiful job of implementing our recommendations. A year after start-up, the plant was in the black, and in three years sales had gone over the million dollar per year mark. In just four short years Elaine had converted a situation that threatened the security of her family into a profitable million-dollar-plus business. Sure she had a lot of help. But in the final analysis, she made the decisions, she lived with the problems, and she made it work, mainly because she had that key ingredient—the desire and motivation to face the situation and see it through. In my mind, Elaine is an outstanding example of what can be accomplished through perseverance and desire.

You can also accomplish a great deal by developing your capabilities through self-motivation and desire. Don't underestimate what can be accomplished. After all, you've already demonstrated enough initiative to read this book. And there are many things you can do right now to better prepare yourself for a business of your own. For example, you should be gathering all the information you can about the key aspects of running any small business. Material relating to management, finance, accounting, bookkeeping, marketing, and so forth will be invaluable when you get started on your own. It's probably a good idea to attend seminars related to small business management and to talk to people with small business experience.

Let your motivation direct your activities in a positive and fruitful manner in both selecting the right business opportunity and in preparing to manage it effectively.

II

SELECTING THE TYPE OF BUSINESS

CHAPTER

5

DEVELOPING A LIST OF POSSIBLE BUSINESS TYPES

To be always intending to live a new life, but
never to find time to set about it; this is as
if a man should put off eating and drinking
and sleeping from one day and night to another,
till he is starved and destroyed.

JOHN TILLOTSON

In this section, we're going to select the type of business that's best suited to you, the one that most nearly matches your business selection criteria and your capabilities. This selection process involves screening a wide variety of possible types of businesses. And that brings us to the purpose of this chapter— developing a comprehensive list of possible business types.

I realize that some people feel that there are only three or four types of businesses that they would be interested in. If you're convinced that you know the types of businesses that you'd be interested in, then you could probably skip developing the list in this chapter. But on the other hand, you might find it worth a few hours of your time to consider some additional possibilities. You'll never know what other possible business types might be worth adding to your list if you don't give it a try.

WHAT TO INCLUDE ON YOUR LIST

In the next part of this chapter, we're going to develop your list of possible types of businesses. But before we start, it's important to

41

understand the guideline for deciding what to include in the list. Fortunately, this guideline is really quite simple; include any type of business where you can say, "Yes, I might like to do that." At this stage it's best to keep your mind open to all appealing possibilities. Don't reject a possibility because you "think" it might not meet your business selection criteria. If in doubt, put it on the list, and then if, in fact, it doesn't meet your criteria, it will be screened out later.

And one more caution, please don't reject any possibilities because you don't feel you have the capabilities necessary for success. Remember, the key to selecting a successful business opportunity is to find one that meets your wants and desires. If you don't possess all the necessary capabilities, you can probably develop them or, for sure, you can hire them. Don't forget, the key to deciding whether to include a type of business on the list is simply to include every possibility that seems appealing. After all, if it doesn't make the list now, it will never have a chance of being selected. So it's important to include even the remotest possibility. Your list can't be too long. The screening process used in the next chapter can handle a list of ten possibilities or a hundred possibilities with equal efficiency.

DEVELOPING YOUR LIST

There are four resources to draw on in developing your list of possible types of businesses. The first is a starter list of possible types of businesses that is presented in Figure 5. Fifty of the most common types of small businesses are included in this list. Review it and use the ones that appeal to you to start your own list on a sheet of paper. The second resource that you can use to add possible business types to your list is the classified telephone directory. The telephone-book yellow pages, in fact, is probably the single most useful source, primarily because it lists just about every product and service offered by small businesses. If you can, use one from a large city, because large ones are usually more comprehensive. Turn to the cross-reference classified index in the front of the yellow pages and then methodically work your way

FIGURE 5
STARTER LIST OF POSSIBLE
TYPES OF BUSINESSES

Retailing

Clothing store
Fashion boutique
Bicycle shop
Bookstore
Antique shop
Camera shop
Art gallery
Drugstore
Stereo shop
Gift shop
Liquor store
Florist
Plant shop
Pet shop
Auto dealership

Food and Recreation

Fast-food franchise
Restaurant
Convenience-store franchise
Bar/cocktail lounge
Boat marina
Riding stable
Campground franchise
Motel

Services

Preschool/day care
Print shop
Landscaping
Rental service
Interior decorating
Warehousing and storage
Home/commercial maintenance
Auto repair franchise
Accounting and tax service
Business services franchise
Car wash
Employment agency
Travel agency
Real estate agency

Industrial

Manufacturing
Machine shop
Distributorship
Wholesaling
Manufacturer's representative
Cartage/delivery

Other

Mail order
Auctioneer
Farming
Artist
Contractor
Restaurant designer
Dog kennel

down the columns. If you find a listing that looks appealing, add it to your list. Additional information on any listing, of course, is available on the page number listed opposite a particular entry. Sometimes you might find it helpful to turn to a particular page in the yellow pages themselves to see how many businesses are listed and what specific aspects of their product or service they are advertising.

I still remember the day I made up my list of possible small business types from a classified telephone directory. I was out of town on business and had had a particularly frustrating day. When I returned to my hotel room, I knew that I had to find a small business activity that would allow me to quit my job. I'm sure I spent over two hours that evening diligently screening the local yellow pages. I still have the list I made. And I consider that evening's work an important step on my way to independence.

Your local public library is a third resource that will be very helpful in adding to your list. In particular, there are four publications that you should review.

- *Standard Rate and Data Service (SRDS) of Business Publications:* This is a directory of business magazines. Just scan the pages and see if any category of magazine or specific magazine title attracts your interest.

- *Thomas Register:* This is a massive eight-volume directory of products. Volume eight is an index to the product categories used in the other seven volumes. Again, just scan through this index and look for products that you might be interested in manufacturing, distributing, or retailing.

- *National Trade and Professional Associations* (Columbia Books): This is a directory of many of the active business associations throughout the country. Rather than scanning all the pages, it's probably best to turn to the key-word index in the book. This index should help to add some more possible business types to your list.

• *Encyclopedia of Associations* (Gale): This is another directory of business associations which will be helpful. Again, the key-word index is the most effective way to use this book.

The fourth and final resource to draw on in developing your list of possible types of businesses is your own background. Review your hobbies, skills, and outside interests for clues to possible businesses. For example, if you're interested in radio-controlled airplanes and model railroading, it would suggest that a hobby shop and manufacturing of airplane- or train-model equipment should be added to your list. And another business possibility that naturally evolves from this same interest area is a sales agency. There are dozens of small hobby-product manufacturers, many of which can't affort full-time sales representatives in some territories. So an interest in hobby products might suggest a manufacturer's representative business opportunity for your list.

Your personal interests can lead to a successful business opportunity. I'm reminded of a friend who has always had a strong interest in women's clothing and fashion. She considered a number of business opportunities and eventually started a maternity boutique with her husband. He has since become involved in other things, and she is happily running her clothing shop.

Once you've isolated your hobbies, skills, and outside interests, it might be a good idea to use the yellow pages to assist in identifying related businesses. Look in the yellow pages for the types of businesses that supply products and services in a specific area of interest. An interest in gardening would lead you directly to landscaping companies, nurseries, florists, and to all the products and services that these businesses offer.

THE FIRST MILESTONE

Well, you've now reached the first milestone in selecting the type of business that's right for you. It really wasn't that painful, was it? I feel a little bit bad about sending you all the way to the library, but there really wasn't any alternative. Anyway, if you haven't used those reference sources before, the exposure to them makes the trip that more worthwhile. Familiarity with several of the reference sources will be helpful later on in the selection process. Besides, if you drove to the library, you may be able to deduct it as a business expense on your income tax.

Somewhere on your list is that special type of business, the one that will get you started on the road to independence. Let's move on to the next chapter, so we can find it.

6

SELECTING YOUR TYPE OF BUSINESS

If one advances confidently in the direction of his dreams, and endeavors to live the life which he has imagined, he will meet with a success unexpected in common hours.

HENRY DAVID THOREAU

Remember the business selection criteria that you developed back in Chapter 2, where you defined your small business goals, the types of work you enjoyed most, and the life-style you were seeking. In this chapter we're going to compare your criteria with your list of possible types of businesses, in order to isolate the one (or maybe more) type of business that comes closest to meeting your goals, work requirements, and life-style desires.

SETTING UP A SCREENING TABLE

The first step in the comparison process is to set up a screening table. I'd suggest you use a fairly large sheet of paper. A ledger sheet would be very good, but any paper that's about 16 inches wide by 11 inches long will do nicely. On your paper, copy the column heading shown on the screening table format guide in Figure 6. Be sure to spread out the ten column headings over the full width of the paper. Also be sure to copy the appropriate number of parentheses under each column heading.

When you've finished making your screening table, you can

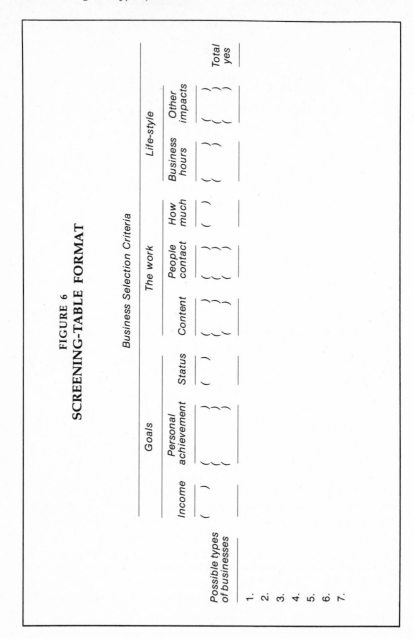

FIGURE 6
SCREENING-TABLE FORMAT

begin to fill in the parentheses under each column. For example, in the parenthesis below the income heading, fill in the dollar income goal you arrived at when developing your business selection criteria. Continue filling in the parentheses under each column heading. Try to use a key word or two to capture the essence of the information on your business selection criteria.

The last step in preparation of screening is to copy your list of businesses from the last chapter under the column headed "Possible Types of Businesses." If you have so many types that they don't fit on the paper, don't worry. Use a second sheet of paper or just tape another sheet of paper to the bottom of your first sheet, and keep listing until you're finished.

THE SCREENING PROCESS

As indicated earlier, the screening process involves comparing your business selection criteria with each of the types of businesses on your list. Basically, the process involves comparing one type of business at a time. Take your first business type and work your way across the page. Put a yes under each column where you feel your criteria is satisfied by that particular type of business. For example, if your income goal is $50,000 a year and you feel that your first business type meets the goal, then put a yes under the income column, opposite that business type. A typical screening table, that has been filled in, is shown in Figure 8.

You might be wondering right now how you're going to complete the table without knowing very much about the type of business on your list. That's a very good question. But if you think about it, you probably know much more about most businesses than you realize. Take the residential real estate business for example. You probably know that the basic function of a real estate business is to sell homes for homeowners. So you should have some idea how this type of business could meet your personal achievement goals. You also are aware of the status of the real estate business. Would a residential real estate business meet your status goals? And then there's the work-related criteria. If you've ever considered buying a home (or selling one), you're probably very familiar with the work involved in real estate sales. It's very people-oriented—from soliciting listings to showing homes and presenting contracts. The function of the business is to get buyers and sellers together. And the work hours, obviously, are mostly when potential buyers are available to look at homes. That means you'd be working evenings and on Saturdays and Sundays if you were in the real estate sales business. So you can assess the impact of business hours and time away from home on your life-style.

Your knowledge and familiarity as a consumer will probably enable you to make fairly accurate appraisals of most businesses. And for decisions at this stage of the business selection process, fair accuracy is good enough. The one column where you may have difficulty is the income column. Very few people have a good intuitive understanding of the income potential of various types of small businesses. In fact, it seems that people in general feel that anybody who owns a business is "making a bundle." That simply isn't true. There are many small business owners that are lucky if they make $5000 to $10,000 a year.

To assist you in deciding whether a particular type of business meets your income goal, Figure 7 has some information on ranges of income for selected types of businesses. Obviously, income for the same type of business varies greatly depending on such things as its size and location, the skill of the management, and the gross margins that can be realized. Therefore, please use this income information only as a guideline in deciding whether to put a yes in the income column. Also note that income is generally related to annual gross sales. If you can operate a business larger than the one shown on the table, you can expect proportionately larger income.

Using the income-range table and your familiarity with the operations and work required for the types of business on your list, you can now complete your screening table for each of the business types in the left-hand column.

When considering a yes entry for each potential type of business, the best way to make a judgment is to envision the actual business environment. Picture the building, the product or ser-

FIGURE 7
INCOME RANGES FOR
SELECTED TYPES OF BUSINESSES

Thousands of dollars

Business type	Starting capital required	Typical annual gross sales	Typical net pre-tax income (owner's salary & profit)
Ice-cream franchise	$ 15–20	$ 90–150	$20–40
Auto repair franchise	25–35	200–300	20–60
Instant printing franchise	20–30	150–250	20–50
Stereo shop	70–80	300–500	25–60
Toy, hobby, or craft shop	40–70	200–300	25–50
Shoe store	50–100	200–300	20–40
Restaurant (100-seat table service)	150–200	200–350	25–50
Pet shop	25–35	75–175	10–30
Dry cleaning	40–80	60–160	10–30
Camera shop	50–100	150–200	15–30
Convenience food store	20–50	100–200	10–35
Home-based maintenance service	10–20	40–100	5–20
Bicycle shop	15–35	75–250	10–50
Apparel store	50–80	200–300	20–40
Manufacturing	20–100	50–1,000	10–100
Distributorship	20–100	100–500	10–60
Mail order	2–20	40–200	10–40
Real estate	10–20	100–500	20–80

vice, your employees and customers. And realize your daily involvement. Then ask yourself the question: Does this business meet my work-content criteria? Or my people-contact criteria? Or my business-hours criteria? By utilizing this process, you can complete your table very effectively. You'll also see why some apparently inconsistent yeses on the sample screening table (Figure 8) are really very logical. For example, in the status column, it would seem that a real estate agency and a travel agency would both offer "moderate" status. But when the person who made these judgments envisioned himself first in a real estate business, then in a travel agency, he logically concluded that, for him, only the real estate business met his status goal.

After you've finished filling in your screening table, you can count up the yeses for each type of business. That is, if your first business type has three yeses (e.g., one in income, one in status, and one in people contact), then enter the number 3 in the far right-hand column. As you enter these totals you'll probably begin to see some interesting results—some business types with mostly all yeses and some with only a few. In the next section, we'll analyze the results and implications of the screening process.

ANALYSIS AND IMPLICATIONS

Well, how do your results look? Do you have one business type that stands out far and above the rest? It's nice to get that kind of result, but it doesn't always happen. More likely you've got two or even three business types that are grouped together with six or seven yeses. What does this kind of result mean? To help you understand and to analyze your results, we're going to examine in detail the sample screening table. By understanding the results and implications of this example, you will be more able to understand your own results.

Let's begin by examining each column on the sample screening table in Figure 8 to see what kind of thinking probably went into the yes responses. In the income column, the person who filled in this table indicated an income goal of $50,000 a year. Notice that

FIGURE 8
SAMPLE SCREENING TABLE

Business selection criteria

Possible types of businesses		Goals		The work			Life-style		Total Yes
	Income ($50,000)	Personal achievement (Minority-group hiring) (Travel)	Status (Moderate)	Content (Hand) (People) (Things)	People contact (All except personal selling)	How much (Eventual) Part-time	Business hours (M–F) (9–5)	Other impacts (10 miles) (No emergency)	
1. Real estate	Yes	No	Yes	No	No	Yes	No	Yes	4
2. Camera shop	No	No	No	Yes	Yes	No	No	Yes	3
3. Bicycle shop	No	No	No	Yes	Yes			Yes	3
4. Lock manufacturing	Yes	Yes	Yes	Yes	No	Yes	Yes	Yes	7
5. Antique shop	Yes	Yes	Yes	Yes	Yes	No	Yes	No	5
6. Dog kennel	No	No	No	No	Yes	No	No	No	1
7. Auto repair franchise	Yes	No	No	Yes	Yes	No	No	No	3
8. Machine shop	Yes	Yes	Yes	Yes	No	Yes	Yes	Yes	7
9. Mail order	Yes	No	Yes	Yes	Yes	Yes	Yes	Yes	7
10. Travel agency	Yes	Yes	No	No	No	No	No	No	2

the person felt that only three businesses did not fulfill this income goal. The one possible surprise here is the dog kennel. Since dog kennel was not on the earlier list of selected income ranges, we might fairly assume that this no is probably somewhat of a guess. But if this guess is wrong, are the results changed? No, they're not, because the total yeses for dog kennel is so low. If the income no were really yes, dog kennel would still have a total score of only 2, which would still leave it out of the running.

Look at the noes in your income column. Would a change of any of them to yes affect the results of your top-scoring business types? If so, circle that no answer so you can recall this for later consideration.

Now let's examine the sample screening table results in the personal-achievement column. Obviously, this is an extremely subjective column. The indicated goals were "minority-group hiring" and "travel." It's interesting to note that the person who filled in the sample table felt that none of the retail type businesses met these personal-achievement goals. Possibly the respondent felt that since retailing is often a local business, there probably would be little travel involved. I'm guessing there's a yes response to travel agency (which is a retail service business) because owners quite frequently arrange group tours and then take on the assignment of tour guide. On the other hand, I can see how the goal of minority hiring could be accomplished in a manufacturing or machine shop environment, which may not involve as much travel. This is our first illustration of subjective ranking of goals. Have you mentally "ranked" any of your personal-achievement goals? If so, note it on your screening table and examine how this ranking has affected your responses in the personal-achievement column.

The status goals, like the personal-achievement goals, are another area where the feelings behind the response are probably more important than the response itself. In our example, the status goal was met by only five of the ten possible businesses. This could be a very significant result, because a no response in the status column of a business type that has a high overall score might mean that you could never accept the "low" status of that particular business type. Circle any noes in the status column of a business type that has a high total score (say 5 yeses or more).

Now let's take a look at the work-content column of the sample screening table. The respondent indicated that seven out of ten business types met his or her work-content goals. And there are yeses for all the business types that have high total scores (i.e., lock manufacturing, antique shop, machine shop, and mail order). Is this the case on your screening table? If not, please circle the noes for high-total-score businesses. The day-in-and-day-out work content is important. So if you don't like a particular type of work, a no might suggest that you should avoid that business.

A similar situation is apparent in the next column of the sample screening table. The respondent indicated that all types of people contact are acceptable, with the exception of personal selling. And that's where a potential problem arises. For two of the person's top-scoring businesses, the lock manufacturing business and the machine shop business, personal selling is essential. For example, if a lock manufacturer can't sell hardware-store purchasing agents or a distributor on a product, then he or she is in serious trouble. So what are the alternatives? The most obvious is to not get involved in these types of businesses. Or possibly, enthusiasm and desire will help overcome the apprehensions associated with personal selling. Another alternative would be to take on a partner who could enthusiastically and energetically carry out the personal-sales function that is an integral part of these types of businesses. Do you have a similar people-contact problem on your screening table? If not, good. If so, circle it for future consideration and also start to consider some alternatives, such as a partner or selling through manufacturer's representatives.

Now let's move on to the "How Much Work" column of our sample screening table. The person who filled in the table indicated a desire to eventually be involved in the business only on a part-time basis. At this stage of our business selection process it is difficult to be sure whether the yeses in this column are accurate. However, there is a good rule of thumb, which it appears was followed by our respondent. The rule is that smaller businesses, like a camera shop or a dog kennel, are generally not able to support both an owner's profits and a manager's salary. Our respondent is probably safe in assuming (and in the next chapter you'll see how to verify this information) that a lock-manufacturing business, a machine shop, and a mail-order business can be built to a size where part-time involvement is possible. If you're interested in something other than permanent full-time involvement, and you're unsure of your yes responses for your high-scoring business types, circle these yeses. Then you can refer back to these circles as we get further along in the analysis.

As you can see on the sample screening table, requiring Monday through Friday, 9 to 5 business hours severely limits the number of businesses where one can indicate a yes response. If you indicated a similar business-hours criteria, and if you have a column full of noes, maybe you should consider modifying your criteria.

The eighth and next-to-last column on the sample screening table is "Other Life-Style Impacts." The person who filled in the table indicated that he or she wanted the business to be within ten miles of home and didn't want to get involved in a business that required customer emergency calls. Since none of the possible types of businesses appear to have an emergency problem, the no responses probably indicate that for some reason, four of the businesses probably cannot be located within a ten-mile radius of the respondent's home. Perhaps there are similar businesses located in this area already. Or maybe the surrounding area is not appropriate for an antique shop or dog kennel. Review your responses in the other-life-style-impact column to make sure you have considered the local competition and the number and buying patterns of potential customers. Site location will be considered in more detail in a later chapter.

Continuing with our examination of the sample screening table, notice that three business types have identical scores. Lock manufacturing, machine shop, and mail order each have a score of 7 yeses. This is an interesting result because these three businesses are really quite different. Lock manufacturing is obviously a business that focuses on a single product. The long-term success of this type of business probably will depend on the design and quality of the lock itself. It's also a business that probably will require a sizable initial capital investment and probably has a national sales potential. And finally, as noted earlier, this business will require a good deal of personal marketing and sales effort.

In contrast, the machine shop business is not at all product-oriented. Most machine shops have a machinery capability which is offered to customers. The customers, who are other manufacturers, use the machine shop to machine specific parts which are then used in the manufacturer's product. So in essence, the machine shop is selling a machining service, not a product. Also, machine shops, in most cases, are local businesses with much less upward sales potential than a lock manufacturer. The one similarity between a lock-manufacturing business and a machine shop is the need for personal-selling capability.

The mail-order business is completely different from both lock manufacturing and a machine shop. To begin with, depending on the products that are sold, there may not be any manufacturing at all. And the most striking difference is that in mail order, there is no direct customer contact, so there is no personal selling.

Thus, in the sample screening table (see Figure 9) we find three completely different businesses, yet each has the same identical total score. This presents somewhat of a dilemma. You may have a similar situation in your own table, but fortunately it can be resolved, as you'll see in the next section of this chapter.

MAKING YOUR INITIAL SELECTION

The results of your screening table may make your selection very obvious. If only one business type has a high total score, then this is probably the business type for you. Identify it as your initial selection. However, it's quite likely that you have three or four business types with high scores, for instance, one with 8 and two with scores of 7. Don't be concerned about this situation. The purpose of this screening process was to take a large number of business types and, by using the business selection criteria, reduce it to a manageable number, say one to four. If you've ac-

FIGURE 9
TABULATION OF INPUTS

Business selection criteria elements	Impor- tance factor	Screening table information		
		Lock manufac- turing	Machine shop	Mail order
Income goal	5	Yes	Yes	Yes
Personal achieve- ment	2	Yes	Yes	No
Status	3	Yes	Yes	Yes
Work content	3	Yes	Yes	Yes
People contact	5	No	No	Yes
How much work	2	Yes	Yes	Yes
Business hours	3	Yes	Yes	Yes
Other life-style impacts	1	Yes	Yes	Yes

complished this you're in good shape. Our next step is to rank your high-scoring business types, so if you don't have a single one that stands out, you can still make an initial selection. And then this initial selection (and possibly one or two of your other high-scoring business types) will be analyzed in detail in the next chapter to verify whether it is indeed the right business for you.

There are two ways to rank your high-scoring business types. The first method is based entirely on your feelings and intuition. The second method is a quantitative approach to ranking your high-scoring business types. You can use the method you prefer. Or you can use both. But I can't guarantee that both will yield the same result, although in most cases they will. If you don't get the same results, I'd recommend that you base your initial selection on your feelings and intuition. After all, many business decisions, in the final analysis, are correctly made based on feelings and intuition.

The feelings-and-intuition method of ranking your high-scoring business types is really quite simple. Just sit back and picture yourself in each type of high-scoring business. Then ask yourself these questions: In which of these businesses would I feel most comfortable? And in which of these businesses would I like to spend the next five, ten, or twenty years of my life? Make your choice. This is your initial business type selection. Put this selection aside. Now repeat the process to select your number-two-ranked business type. You've now got your runner-up business type selected. If you initially had four high-scoring business types, repeat the process once more, so you'll end up with a number one, two, and three ranking of business types.

The second method, the quantitative approach, is not quite as simple, but it is an enlightening and informative ranking system. This system is related directly to the eight elements of the business selection criteria. It recognizes that these elements are not of equal importance and that the relative importance of each element varies from person to person. For example, to some people, the income and personal-achievement goals will be most important, while to others, the work and impact-on-life-style elements might overshadow income and personal achievement.

This method is best illustrated with an example. You may recall that on the sample screening table, three business types (lock manufacturing, machine shop, and mail order) had identical total scores of seven yeses. Let's try to rank these three by using the quantitative approach. The first step is to develop an importance factor for each of the elements. This is done on a scale of one to five, with one indicating a low importance factor and five a high importance factor. Two, three, and four are used to indicate relative importance factors between low and high. Assume, for example, that the person who filled out the sample screening table made the following importance-factor assignment (these assignments are made based on personal preference).

High importance (5)	*Average importance* (3)	*Below-average importance* (2)	*Low importance* (1)
Income	Status	How much work	Other
People contact	Work content	Personal	impacts
	Business hours	achievement	

The next step in the process is to tabulate the importance-factor assignment and the screening-table information for each of the business types being ranked, as shown in Figure 9. Now the final step is to place the proper numerical importance factor next to each yes for each business type as shown in Figure 10. (I realize that this appears to be getting rather complicated, but you'll see shortly that it's really not that bad):

FIGURE 10
TOTALING IMPORTANCE FACTORS

Business selection criteria element	Lock manufac- turing	Machine shop	Mail order
Income goal	Yes— 5	Yes— 5	Yes— 5
Personal achieve- ment	Yes— 2	Yes— 2	No
Status	Yes— 3	Yes— 3	Yes— 3
Work content	Yes— 3	Yes— 3	Yes— 3
People contact	No	No	Yes— 5
How much work	Yes— 2	Yes— 2	Yes— 2
Business hours	Yes— 3	Yes— 3	Yes— 3
Other life-style impacts	Yes— 1	Yes— 1	Yes— 1
Totals	19	19	22

Totaling of the yes importance factors results in a higher total score for the mail-order business type. You can see from the table above that this outcome was a result of the high importance factor of five that was assigned to the people-contact element, which says that, to this person, the type of people contact (all except personal selling) was the decisive factor. This quantitative method pinpointed the mail-order business, which has no personal selling, as the initial business type selection.

Another interesting result of this method is that lock manufacturing and machine shop have identical totals. The obvious reason for this is that they have identical screening-table responses. And this is where any systematic approach fails to work. The screening and selection process ranked both businesses very highly, but it can not differentiate between them, even though, as we saw earlier, these two businesses are in fact very different in their nature and potential. So feelings and intuition, in the final analysis, will have to be used in this example to select the second-highest-ranking business type.

If you have several high-scoring business types, it's time now to rank them so you can make your initial business type selection. Use the method you feel most comfortable with. You'll see in the next chapter that by gathering and analyzing a good deal of information on a specific type of business, you'll be well equipped to confirm or reject your initial selection.

Remember the suggestion that you circle certain responses on your screening table, if appropriate. Well, if you have any of these circled, now's the time to take another look at them. Are any of the circles associated with the initial selection you just made? If so, recall the reason for the circle, and try to keep it in mind when you analyze your initial selection in the chapter. This will help direct your analysis and assist in raising appropriate questions.

THE IMPORTANCE OF ENTHUSIASM

There's one last item that should be covered before going ahead to the next chapter—it's the matter of enthusiasm and excitement that it is hoped you feel about your selection. Do you feel enthusiastic about the choice you just made? Are you excited about its future potential? If you are, that's great! You're ready to proceed. But if you're not, maybe something's wrong, and it's possible that the something that's wrong is that you haven't identified the right business, not because of an error in the screening process, but because that right business somehow wasn't on the list you developed in the last chapter.

I can readily identify with this predicament, because I found myself in the same situation. I had made up what I thought to be a comprehensive list. Then I screened it against my business selection criteria. None of the business types had a really high score. And to make matters worse I wasn't really excited about the initial selection that resulted. I decided to proceed with the detailed analysis anyway, yet at the same time I kept my antennas up and was constantly alert for new possible business types to add to my list.

If you lack enthusiasm and excitement, I suggest you do the same thing. Go on to the next chapter where you'll see how to analyze your present business selection, but also keep your eyes and ears open for new possible business types. Constantly be on the alert for new ideas. Explore every one of your waking experiences for new possibilities. When you hit on one, and you will, add it to your screening table. Then send it through the screening process to see how it stacks up. If it looks good, and you're enthusiastic about it, then apply the techniques described in the next chapter to verify your findings.

7

ANALYZING YOUR SELECTION BY GETTING THE FACTS

*I had six honest serving men—they taught
me all I knew: Their names were Where and
What and When—and Why and How and Who.*

RUDYARD KIPLING

Well, you've already made great progress in your search for a small business opportunity that offers a high probability of success. You've narrowed down a diverse list of business types to an initial selection and several other high-ranking possibilities. In this chapter, you'll see how some relatively simple business research and analysis techniques can be used to verify your selection—or reject it if necessary.

Specifically, this chapter is designed to accomplish three objectives:

1. To develop enough detailed information about your selection to see if it does, in fact, satisfy most of the wants and desires you seek in a business of your own. That is, does your selection meet your business selection criteria:

Goals

- Income

- Personal achievement

- Status

The Work

- Content

- People contact

- How much

Life-Style

- Business hours

- Other impacts

2. To determine the attributes and capabilities that are required to succeed in the business you've selected:

- Health and physical capabilities

- Educational requirements

- Specific experience

- Managerial skills

- Technical requirements

- Marketing and sales skills

- Investment capabilities

3. To assess the current condition and outlook for your selected business type:

- Earnings potential

- Current profitability

- Past and future growth

- Owner's satisfactions or regrets

SOURCES OF INFORMATION

Obviously, much information will be required to fulfill the objectives of this chapter. Where will it all come from? Well, there are several sources, each serving a different purpose. In this section, four basic sources of information will be described. In addition, techniques useful in identifying business information sources are pointed out.

Remember the association directories you used to help generate your list of possible business types? Many of the associations listed in these directories are valuable sources of information. You can use the key-word index of the directory to identify the associations that are involved in your business-interest area. For example, if your initial business selection is auto repair franchise, look in the key-word index under *automobile* and *franchise*. You'll find a listing of associations that could be helpful: Automotive Transmission Rebuilders Association, Automotive Engine Rebuilders Association, Automotive Market Research Council, National Automotive Muffler Association, National Automotive Parts Association, and the International Franchise Association.

The second major source of information is magazines and trade publications. You're already familiar with the most comprehensive directory of business publications, the *Standard Rate and Data Service Directory of Business Publications*. You used it, along with the association directories, in developing your list of business types. This directory is organized into major categories of publications. So if you're interested in the auto repair area, for example, look in the automotive section. You'll find an almost unbelievable number and variety of publications. Some that are in the auto repair area are *Automotive Aftermarket News, Automotive Service and Body News, Automotive Rebuilder, Brake and Front End Service,* and *Service Station Management*. Always note the name, address, and phone number of the publisher; it's generally different from the name of the magazine. Also copy down the names of several of the editors. You'll want to direct your inquiry for information to one of these editors.

A third source of information is most appropriately called miscellaneous. The Small Business Administration, a U.S. government agency, is a major source of miscellaneous information. This information includes free publications and "for-sale" booklets. Another invaluable miscellaneous source is financial institutions. The primary example is the Bank of America publication entitled *Small Business Reporter,* which offers about thirty reports, each of which profiles a different small business. And they also have about fifteen reports on various small business operations and problem areas (e.g., advertising, avoiding management pitfalls, etc.). Surprisingly, each of these reports is available for only $1. Subscription rates and reprint information is available by writing Small Business Reporter, Department 3120, P.O. Box 37000, San Francisco, CA 94137.

There are thousands and thousands of newsletters published every month. Some of these could be very useful sources of information. You'll find them listed by subject in the *National Directory of Newsletters and Reporting Services* at your local library. Many times, back issues or a trial subscription is available at a modest charge.

The final miscellaneous source of information is books. Besides directories, your local public or college library probably has many books that could be helpful. Look in the card file under the subjects you're interested in, and don't hesitate to ask the librarian for all the help you need.

The fourth and best source of information is small business owners. They're right out there on the firing lines every day, so they know what's going on. And they'll tell you even though you're a possible future competitor. The art of gathering information and opinions from business owners is covered later in this chapter.

GETTING INFORMATION FROM TRADE ASSOCIATIONS

Trade Associations are useful sources of several different types of information. Some associations have market research or statistical departments which produce very informative reports. Associations at times also have technical people who carry out member-sponsored research. Most associations publish booklets describing the activities of the association and its members. And finally, almost all associations publish membership directories. These directories are extremely useful in locating small businesses and determining the name of the owner or manager.

One word of caution. Some associations have a policy which prevents them from distributing certain types of information to nonmembers. Sometimes you can get around this roadblock by obtaining association publications directly from a member. You'll probably run across members when you're talking to them as business owners. Remember to ask them for extra copies of any association publication they might have.

If you're lucky enough to find an association you're interested in within commuting distance of your home, I'd recommend you visit them personally. You'll want to see the association managers—the executive director, secretary, or vice-president. In a large association, an assistant or department head could also be helpful. You'll find the names of the right people in the association directory. Phone in advance to make an appointment. Just say you're interested in business opportunities in such and such a field and you would like to chat about it, at the manager's convenience. Most times, he or she will be happy to see you.

Personal visits are probably not possible in most cases. If that's the situation, a phone discussion or letter makes a good substitute. If you call and the manager seems in a hurry, suggest that you call back when the person has more time to chat. Ask the manager to suggest a convenient time, and then be sure to call at that time. A letter should be addressed to the executive director (or whatever the title is) and should briefly describe your purpose and the kind of information you're seeking. For example:

Dear Mr. (Ms.) ———,

I'm interested in a possible business opportunity in the automotive repair field. I understand that your association may have some information in this area. Would you please send me any information you can. I'm specifically interested in:

- Specifications and catalogs

- Market research reports

- Product literature

- Membership requirements

- Membership directories

Also, I've attached a list of questions that you may be able to help me answer.

Thank you for your assistance. I greatly appreciate it.

Sincerely,

P.S. Could you suggest any other people in the industry whom I might contact?

The list of questions attached to this letter will be basically the same as the list you'll develop for your discussions with business owners. Suggestions on preparing this list are covered in a later section of this chapter, entitled "Getting Information from Business Owners."

GETTING INFORMATION FROM PUBLICATIONS

Publishers of business magazines can supply you with some valuable information. Besides the material that's in the magazine itself, some larger publishers have market research departments which at various times publish very useful quantitative booklets and reports. Business magazine publishers also typically publish special issues of their magazines. A very common special issue is called a buyer's guide, which lists the products an industry usually purchases and the suppliers of each type of product. For example, a magazine serving the restaurant equipment industry might publish an annual restaurant equipment buyer's guide. It would list everything from steam tables to pots and pans. For someone whose initial business selection is a restaurant, a restaurant equipment buyer's guide could be very helpful in collecting supplier's names and equipment descriptions.

Some business magazine publishers also issue separate industry directories. Typical examples are *The Packaging Encyclopedia* (for the food packaging industry) and the *Fluid Power Handbook* (for the hydraulics industry). Many of these directories are just packed with invaluable and sometimes very detailed information. These directories are usually listed in the *Standard Rate and Data Service Directory of Business Publication* in conjunction with the corresponding magazine listing.

As was true with trade associations, a personal visit is probably the best way to gather information from a business magazine publisher. Call one of the editors, explain your purpose, and request an appointment. This personal visit will allow you to see the special issues and directories before you purchase them. But more importantly, it will present the perfect setting to ask the editor all the questions you have on the industry served by the publication. Many magazine editors are very knowledgeable and helpful.

If a personal visit is not possible, a phone call to an editor to ask questions will probably do nicely. You may even be sent several complementary issues of the magazine. A letter can also be used to ask your questions and order publications. When ordering magazines, I'd suggest requesting the last six issues, rather than a subscription. This approach will give you six months of information without waiting six months. You can always order a subscription at a later date if your interest in the publication continues.

GETTING INFORMATION FROM THE GOVERNMENT

The focal point of federal government small business information and assistance is the Small Business Administration (SBA). The SBA is an independent agency of the government whose sole purpose is to help small businesses. This agency has eighty-six field offices that offer financial and management assistance, aid in obtaining government contracts, counseling services, and over two hundred publications covering many small business types and practices. Much of this is free of charge.

The SBA "Free Management Assistance Publications" (SBA

Form 114a) includes a listing of about 150 different publications available free from the SBA. These publications include a series of Management Aids, Technical Aids, Small Marketing Aids, and Small Business Bibliographies. A list and order form of "For-sale Booklets" (SBA Form 115b) is also available. This list includes the Small Business Management Series, the Starting and Managing Series, the Small Business Research Series, and a small group of miscellaneous publications. For-sale booklets are often no more than $1 and the most expensive is less than $3.

The most appropriate first step in developing a relationship with the SBA is to phone the nearest field office and ask that a listing of the free and for-sale publications be sent to you. Look them over and then order the ones that seem appropriate. Some titles are quite similar to those of the Bank of America *Small Business Reporter*. However, in most cases the SBA papers and the *Small Business Reporter* complement each other. Since both groups of publications are so modestly priced, you probably should order from both sources.

Another appropriate step in information gathering is a personal visit to your SBA office. Call to make an appointment to see someone who is experienced in an area related to the business type you're probing. This meeting could be very worthwhile.

As you get further along in establishing a small business of your own, you'll probably want to take advantage of other resources offered by the SBA. These include SBA loans, economic opportunity loans, economic development loans, disaster loans, lease guarantee plans, small business investment companies, SCORE (Service Corps of Retired Executives), management courses, conferences, workshops, clinics, foreign trade, technology utilization, and government procurement assistance.

GETTING INFORMATION FROM BUSINESS OWNERS

It's time to go to the firing line, the small business owners. You might be somewhat apprehensive about this step. That's normal, but really you shouldn't be. After all, business owners are people, just like you and me. And even more importantly, you can't afford not to talk to business owners. The best way to find out if you want to be in a certain type of business is to talk to people who have been there. Shying away from this source of information and opinion is like buying a new car without asking present owners what they think of theirs. Actually it's a more serious mistake—a car is just a car. If it's not right, you can tolerate it or trade it. But a business is not just a business. It's your livelihood and a good deal of your life. So find out before you invest.

Before you can talk to business owners, you're going to have to identify them. For most types of businesses, this can easily be done by looking in the yellow pages. Copy on a sheet of paper the names, addresses, and phone numbers of eight or ten of the companies. By taking some with large ads and some with brief listings, you'll probably get a good cross section of business sizes. And while you've got the book open, study the ads. Look at the approaches. Notice what's being emphasized. Is it quality, service, reliability, long hours of service, or something else? Then when you visit a particular business owner, you can casually say, "I noticed in your yellow pages' ad you emphasize your company's experience. Exactly how important to the customer is experience?" The owner will be flattered that you remembered the ad and will realize that you're interested enough in the business to take note of such things.

There are two other good ways to identify businesses. The first is the names you may have gotten in your visit to the SBA and the second is in the information you collected from trade associations. If you have a membership directory or two, these can be very useful because often they list people's names and titles within the company listing.

We now arrive at the issue of whom to talk to in a small business. If the business is very small and the owner is in fact carrying out most of the functions of the business alone, that's the person you'll want to see. Probably there isn't anybody else in authority. In somewhat larger small businesses, you have some choice. There's the owner, of course, but there is also a sales manager, a controller, and a production manager. You very likely want either the owner or the sales manager. Finance and production people generally have only an inward view of the business, while most of the questions that you're seeking answers to are about the business environment and outlook. So try for the owner, and if it can't be arranged, ask to see the sales manager.

It's important to meet small business owners in a setting that's private, quiet, and as free from interruptions as possible. If the person you're seeing has a private office, that's usually the best place. But many small business owners don't have such facilities, so you should find a suitable substitute. Meeting for lunch or a cup of coffee in a quiet restaurant is always a good approach. Inviting the owner to your home may work out, or you may even be invited to his or her home. A final possibility is to suggest meeting for a drink or dinner. I've always found one-on-one discussions at dinner to be informative. The atmosphere is very relaxed, and there is always plenty of time to weave all the questions into the discussion.

You might wonder at this point what to say when you phone a business owner for an appointment. And you're probably curious why this person would agree to see you when you do call. Let's take these questions one at a time. Your approach in calling for an appointment should be informal, relaxed, and direct. Part of the informality may be to call the business owner by his or her first name. After exchanging "How are you's," you can go directly to your reason for calling. Always try to minimize the "threat" to the owner's business when explaining why you want an appointment. For example, if the person operates an auto repair shop on the north side of a large city, explain that you're interested in possibly opening a shop in the far south suburbs (20 to 25 miles away and well beyond the owner's market area).

Of course, you always should be truthful. So if you're planning a shop on the north side, you'll probably be better off calling shop owners in the far south suburbs. Then you can honestly and in good conscience minimize the threat by saying you're considering opening a shop on the north side. If you're planning to start your business in a relatively small town, you might have to call business owners in a town twenty miles away to be able to honestly say that you're not threatening their business.

Here's an approach I use in arranging appointments:

Person answering phone: Good morning, XYZ Company.

Me: Good morning. My name is Ken Albert. I'm trying to locate the owner of XYZ, but I don't know his name.

Person: That's Mr. Jones. I'll transfer . . .

Me: What is his first name?

Person: Ed Jones.

Me: Thank you.

Person: Transferring.

Ed Jones: Hello.

Me: Is this Mr. Ed Jones?

Ed Jones: Speaking.

Me: Ed, my name is Ken Albert. How are you today?

Ed Jones: Oh, not bad.

Me: Ed, I'm interested in possibly opening up an auto repair shop in Elmhurst, and I'm trying to arrange to talk to some shop owners to get a better feel for the business. I wonder if I could make an appointment to see you sometime.

Ed Jones: Well, this is a very busy month for us.

Me: How about if I call you in a month or so? I can either come to your office or we could meet for lunch or something.

Ed Jones: Ya, O.K. I might be able to tell you a few things. Call me for lunch sometime.

Me: Real good. Thanks, Ed. I'll be in touch.

Ed Jones: Good-bye.

There, we did it. Now that wasn't too hard, was it? But what if Ed continued to make excuses or flat out refused? Well, that does happen once in a while, and you'll just have to roll with it. Insurance salesmen do it all the time. They estimate that out of every ten prospects, they sell an average of one policy. They're used to hearing the word *no,* yet they just keep forging ahead. Your success ratio will be much better than one in ten, probably more like six or eight out of ten.

Why did Ed agree to see me next month? I'm really not sure, but I can guarantee you that most people will. Maybe he's just a friendly, outgoing person. Or possibly he sees the meeting as an ego trip, where he'll get a chance to show off his knowledge of the business. Or perhaps he thinks that since you're talking to other owners, he'll be able to get some competitive information from you. This brings us to a little incentive you can give a business owner to see you. When you're explaining your purpose, tack on something like this: "I've been making quite an extensive evaluation of the auto repair shop business. All in all, I'm talking to about ten shop owners. One reason I'd like to see you is to get your reaction to some of the things I've heard." That should perk up his interest. If he wants to know what kind of things you're referring to, just say, "Well, they're fairly complicated issues, so I'd rather not go into them on the phone." What you're doing is offering to trade information. It's done every day by consultants who are doing business research for large companies. And it's completely ethical as long as you don't disclose any confidential information or quote directly any of your other sources.

And you really don't have to trade very much. If I were to see Ed, I might offer a few tidbits such as, "I've heard from several shop owners that they're really worried about a possible crackdown by the city consumer protection department. What is your reaction?" Here you're turning a bit of vague information for him into a valuable question for you. He feels as though he's learned something, and you're receiving answers to your questions.

When considering the best approach to asking questions, there are several guidelines. First, you should have your questions written down. You can list them on a sheet of paper and write your notes on a separate pad. Or you can spread them out over five or six sheets of paper and write your notes under the appropriate question. The second guideline has just been covered. That is, always take notes during the discussion! The business owners won't mind. Just pull out your notebook and pen the first time they say something you want to remember. They will notice you doing it, but chances are they won't say anything about it. And if they do, just explain by saying: "I hope you don't mind. I have a terrible memory. I'd just like to take a few notes for my own use." A few minutes later they will have gotten used to the idea and will be as open and cooperative as ever.

The next guideline concerns the tone and flavor of the discussion. Notice I use the word *discussion*. The meeting should be as close to a discussion as possible. Try to develop a relaxed, confident, and informal exchange of ideas. A pure question-and-answer session may make the business owner feel uncomfortable and uneasy. It's best to control the discussion by keeping the person on the topic and then weaving in your questions when appropriate.

Another guideline involves the order of the questions. Arrange the questions on your list so that the easy ones come first, and try as much as possible to ask them in this order.

A final guideline on the method of asking questions—try to phrase them clearly and concisely. Then listen to the answer. Now probe for more detail and explanations. Interject a "Why is that?" or a "How did that come about?" or "Could you explain that to me?" Another good tactic to use after an answer is given is silence. Plain old silence. Often there's more to be said, and silence will draw it out. Chances are he or she will say something very interesting after a few seconds. I remember a discussion I had with a marketing manager of a medium-sized company. I asked how profitability in the industry had changed in the last few years, and he said, "Well, it hasn't been getting any better." I looked at him in silence and then he blurted out, "As a matter of fact, we're on the verge of declaring bankruptcy." I immediately said, "I'm sorry to hear that. What's the problem?" And he said, "The new Japanese technology has been killing us." So you see, with a little silence and a probing "What's the problem?" I went from knowing only that profitability wasn't getting any better to knowing that this company was being killed by new foreign technology. And, of course, I followed up with the question "Could you explain the new Japanese technology to me?" And he did!

One last point on question asking. Don't hesitate to ask the hard questions. But do save them until the end of the meeting. Then you have nothing to lose if the person is offended. A typical hard question would be "How much can a person make in a year in a business this size?" If the answer is too evasive, then ask, "Would you mind telling me how much you make per year?" It's worth a chance; someone might just tell you.

Once in a while you're going to be successful in arranging an appointment, but the business owner will turn out to be uncooperative. The person may be having a bad day or maybe just feels that there's nothing in it for him or her and so won't go along. Don't let this bother you. As the old saying goes, "There are a lot of fish in the sea." Simply shrug these things off and move on to the next meeting.

You may feel somewhat hesitant about your first meeting or two, especially since you won't have the knowledge and confidence that a few good discussions will give you. You're not alone. It's quite common for newly hired management consultants to sit at their desks for a week, massaging trade association statistics in order to delay their first meeting "until they know more about the industry." Some preparation is fine, but it can be overdone. I've found that the best way to get wet is to just dive in. Your first several meetings may be a little rough, but then you'll be fine.

The whole emphasis of this section has been on personal visits to business owners. That's because it's really the only effective way to do it. Sometimes, however, personal meetings are not possible. In mail order, for example, the businesses are scattered all over the country, as you'll see if you scan the home-shopper section of *Better Homes and Gardens*. Travel expenses to visit these companies would probably be prohibitive. So your next best choice is the telephone. Explain that you'd like to visit in person but that it's not possible. If necessary, call back to ask your questions at the business owner's convenience.

A third method of gathering information from business owners is by letter. My experience has not been very positive in this area.

First, you'll be lucky if two or three owners out of ten respond. Second, the information you receive will be fairly superficial. Finally, there's no way of asking the probing "how" and "why" questions that are possible in a personal or phone conversation. My advice is to avoid using the mail unless there is no alternative.

The last topic in this section is the list of questions to ask business owners. Obviously this list of questions is not the same for each business type, but there is a common foundation. That common foundation is the objectives that are listed on the first page of this chapter. These objectives are the reason for all the information gathering from business owners. It might be well to quickly look back at these objectives on page 63. Listed below (with "easy" questions first) are some basic questions which apply to most business types. When reading this list, keep the objectives in mind and add whatever questions are necessary to answer these objectives for the specific type of business you're evaluating.

Basic Questions for Business Owners

Life-Style

1. What are the hours the business is open?

2. How much additional time does the owner put in?

3. How much "free time" does the owner have each week?

4. Are there any other life-style impacts of this particular business?

The Work Involved

5. Specifically, what does the business owner's work involve? Percent spent in each activity?

6. What are the types and extent of people contact?

Goals

7. How does the owner view the status of the business? Why?

8. What are the owner's personal goals? Does the business supply the opportunity (or free time) to accomplish them? Why? Why not?

Attributes and Capabilities Required for Success

9. Does the business require any unusual physical capability or stamina? In what way?

10. Are there any specific educational requirements that are essential? Helpful?

11. What is the specific work experience of the owner? Is this background necessary for success?

12. What managerial skills are required? (Ask the person to illustrate and elaborate.) Why?

13. Is any specific technical knowledge required for success? What kinds?

14. What marketing and sales skills are required? How involved is the owner in sales calls, promotion, advertising, and other sales activities?

15. How much capital did the owner have to start (or buy) the business? How much would be recommended now? How would the initial capital be allocated (equipment, inventory, salaries, etc.)?

Current Conditions and Outlook

16. What is the average size in gross sales of businesses like the owner's? Is that about average?

17. Is the business growing? At what percent per year? Is this growth slower or faster than five years ago? Why? How much have prices been

increasing each year? (Remember, if dollar sales are up 5 percent in a year, but prices are up 7 percent, that's a 2 percent shrinkage in real growth).

18. What kind of growth is expected in the future? Why?

19. Is the owner satisfied with this type of business? Would the owner start the same type of business if he or she were to do it today? Why? Why not?

20. What things are in store for this type of business five to ten years down the road? Why?

21. What is the earnings potential for an average-size business of this type? How does that break down into profit and owner's salary? Could the owner give some idea of his or her earnings last year?

You should expect to answer all these questions. And I guarantee that if you visit enough owners (probably about ten) and ask all the questions in a friendly and polite manner, you'll get results. To illustrate what can be accomplished, I'm going to show you some information that was developed through owner interviews. Figure 11 shows an income statement for the average skin-care salon. Actually, the information on this income statement is much more specific and detailed than the information you'll be seeking. But it illustrates very well the type of information that can be developed.

ANALYZING YOUR INFORMATION

When you've gathered all the information needed, you'll have a wide variety of facts and opinions from six or more sources:

- Trade associations
- Publications
- Newsletters

- *Small Business Reporter* (Bank of America)
- SBA
- Business owners

FIGURE 11
SKIN-CARE SALON
AVERAGE INCOME STATEMENT

	Dollars	*Percent*
Gross Sales	$130,000	100
Services—$65,000		
Products—$65,000		
Direct Costs		
Labor	20,000	16
Products	43,500	33
Commissions	6,500	5
Overhead, taxes, etc.	19,600	15
Total costs	89,600	69
Net after taxes		
(including owner's salary)	$ 40,400	31

The next step is to put all this information into an organized form so that you can use it to make a decision. Probably one of the best ways to do this is to take three sheets of 8½ × 11 lined paper. On the top of the first sheet, write the following question:

- Does this business type satisfy most of the wants and desires (that is, the business selection criteria) I am seeking in a business?

Under this question, on about 3 lines, summarize your business selection criteria. On the top of page 2, write this question:

- Do I have or can I develop (or hire) the attributes and capabilities that are required for success in this business?

Below this, on several lines, summarize your capabilities assessment guide developed in Chapter 3. Finally, on the top of the third sheet of paper, write this question:

- Is the current condition and outlook for this business type good?

Now you'll want to systematically sort through all the information you've collected. When you run across a key finding that relates to one of the questions on your sheets of paper, briefly summarize it on the appropriate page. Continue to do this until you've sorted through all your information, especially the notes from your business-owner visits. If necessary, add a second sheet of paper behind the question page.

You've now got everything condensed and organized. Is the information complete enough and consistent enough to make your judgment? It may be or it may not be. You'll have to decide. But if you feel a need for additional information or clarification, don't worry. You have another step you can take. It's known as "call-backs" in the consulting trade, and the name just about describes it. Just call back an association director, magazine editor, or business owner and say, "Hi! Remember me? I was in to see you (or called you, or wrote you) several weeks ago. Well, I've just been going over my notes and I have a few things I don't understand. I wonder if you could help me out?" Then ask your questions. Since you are now known from the previous contact, the person will probably be very helpful. If you have conflicts in your information, you can even handle this with a call-back. For example, say something such as: "There's one thing that's been troubling me. When I asked you about profits, you said they averaged about 10 percent after taxes. But several other owners said they were only netting about 3 percent. Can you explain the difference?" It may have been that the owner was exaggerating and, now realizing how much you know, may back down. Or you may be given a legitimate reason why this business does better than average. Either way you'll have resolved the conflict.

There is one other decision you'll have to make about the validity of your information. Simply stated, you must decide, using your best judgment, "who to believe" or "what to believe" when there is an inconsistency. Don't make the mistake of believing some statistical information just because it's been published by a government agency, trade association, or magazine. All these sources, from time to time, print information that is completely misleading or invalid. Generally speaking, if you get the same answer to a question from three or more independent sources, it's probably believable. If you have conflicting information from two sources, tend to believe the person who logically explains "why" or "how" their opinion was developed.

When you've finished your information gathering and organization, it's time for you to do some serious thinking. Ponder the three questions on the top of your pages of paper and also the information on the rest of the paper. This information should allow you to make a sound decision, to verify whether your initial business type selection is valid or to reject the selection. The decision may be obvious—if the facts and opinions are mostly positive or mostly negative. But if you're somewhere in the broad middle ground, don't make a hasty judgment. Give it some time. Discuss the issues with your spouse and with friends. Then, if necessary, give it some more thought.

A PEP TALK

I realize that the fact gathering and analysis described in this chapter is not easy. It requires a good deal of work and initiative on your part. But "getting the facts" is extremely important. A sound decision *cannot* be made without them, so don't hesitate. Dive right in and get to work, and you'll be glad you did. Don't worry about being a little ill at ease during your first few visits with people. They'll understand. We once hired a new consultant who was ill at ease and got off to a terrible start. He arranged his first meeting with a trade association director. The director's secretary showed him into the office, he shook hands, and sat down. After exchanging pleasantries about the weather, he began to ask his first question. But at the same time he unconsciously leaned back too far in his chair and fell over. Now that's getting off to a bad start! But he took it in stride and completed the project in excellent fashion. It's not important how you start, only that you do start.

CHAPTER

8

ARE YOU READY TO
MAKE A COMMITMENT?

When confronted with two courses of action I jot down
on a piece of paper all the arguments in favor of each
one—then on the opposite side I write the arguments
against each one. Then by weighing the arguments
pro and con and canceling them out, one against the
other, I take the course indicated by what remains.

BENJAMIN FRANKLIN

You're now at a key decision point in the business selection process. You must decide whether to commit yourself to the business type you just analyzed. If you decide to commit, then you can go ahead with the process of selecting a specific business opportunity in that business type. For example, if you've just analyzed auto repair shops and you've decided to commit to that type of business, you can now proceed with selecting a specific auto repair shop opportunity.

However, if for some reason, and the possible reasons are endless, you decide against a commitment at this time, you're really saying, "I'm not sure my initial selection is right for me." Or you might be saying, "I *know*, based on the information I gathered, that my initial selection is not right for me." In either case, the thing to do is to go back to the ranking process that was completed at the end of Chapter 6. Find the second-ranked business on the list and send it through the fact gathering and analysis process of Chapter 7.

When this process is completed on your second-ranking business type, you'll have a great deal of information on two types of businesses. By putting them side by side you'll be able to highlight the differences. And by seeing the differences, you'll probably feel much more comfortable in selecting one of them.

I really hesitate to bring up this point, but there is one more possibility. It's possible that you may decide, after analyzing your second-ranking business type, that neither your second-ranking nor your initially selected business type is right for you. Then what do you do? Well, there is only one alternative: go back and send your third-ranking business type through the fact gathering and analysis process of Chapter 7. I know this sounds like a very tedious process. And I hope it won't happen to you. In most cases, analysis of the third-ranked business type is not necessary.

However, many people do go back to analyze their second choice. If you feel that you want to, or need to do this, I can sympathize with you. I did the same thing. My initial business type selection was a residential real estate agency, and when I began the analysis of this selection, I was very enthusiastic. In fact, I was so sure that it was the business for me that I enrolled in a course to prepare for my broker's examination. I completed my initial fact-gathering work with trade associations and publications, and I was still enthusiastic. So I launched into visits with real estate brokers. Then something began to happen. It happened slowly, and I think my enthusiasm blinded me to it for a while. But gradually I was becoming more and more aware of the impact this business would have on my life-style. Evening and weekend work was a way of life for many of the brokers I talked to. In fact, several of them couldn't see me on weekends because of appointments they had made to show property. Younger brokers, who were just getting started, were working almost every evening and on weekends. I was very positive about this business except for the business hours' impact on my life-style. In the final analysis, that factor made me decide that residential real estate was not for me. I just couldn't see myself sacrificing so much of my family life.

So there I was with a negative decision on my initial business selection. Well, second on my list of business types was the mail-order business. I began to gather information on this business type. First I spoke to trade associations and publishers. Then I met with about seven mail-order business owners. One of the owners was a little more cooperative than I had expected. He and his wife and I met for dinner, where he not only told me everything I wanted to know about the business, but also offered to sell me *his* business! You'll find that this will happen once in a while. But be careful of overanxious sellers. It may mean the business is in trouble.

In my discussions with mail-order business owners, I discovered one characteristic of the business that didn't appeal to me. This characteristic was the total emphasis of most companies on building a catalog and a list of names and addresses to send it to. For the most part, companies placing the ads that you see in the mail-order shopping section of magazines do not even break even on them. The primary purpose of these ads is to identify (by soliciting an initial order) people who shop by mail. The name and address on the order is then added to the catalog mailing list. Then the catalogs are sent out to this list three or four times a year, in hopes of generating large multiple-item orders. These large-dollar catalog orders generate the profit for the business. I had hoped when I initially began investigating the mail-order business to specialize in one product and to sell it using magazine advertising. The information I developed in my business-owner visits suggested that this possibility was remote. And somehow, I just couldn't see myself getting involved with an ever-changing, computer-controlled list of hundreds of thousands of names and a thirty-six-page catalog of household gadgets.

Fortunately, some mail-order businesses do rely on a single product and magazine advertising. They can succeed because they offer a unique, sometimes patented, product that can generate enough sales volume to support the business. Products such as mailbox markers and air-inflated "waterbeds" fall into this category. I decided this was the type of mail-order business for me; it met most of my business selection criteria, I felt I had the necessary capabilities, and the future of this business appeared healthy. There was one problem, however. I didn't have a unique, let alone patented, product.

So the results of the analysis of my second-ranking choice were positive, yet inconclusive. I found that I was not attracted to the typical catalog-type mail-order operation. Fortunately, I also discovered a little niche in the mail-order business (selling a unique single product) that looked right for me, if I had the right product. I hope you too will have a positive result if you find it necessary to screen your second-ranking business type.

As indicated in the Introduction, large companies quite frequently hire management consulting firms to analyze new business opportunities. Even these giants don't seem to have any "magic formula" for making good initial selections. In fact, large companies, more often than not, decide against getting involved in the initial business they request the management consultants to analyze. And some of these companies examine five or ten business types before making a selection. This is especially true of large companies who are searching for business opportunities that are completely foreign to their present operations.

I once worked as a consultant for a large company whose main business activity was supplying large stampings and forgings to auto and truck manufacturers. Initially, this company felt that building products would be a great diversification opportunity. The specific product they had in mind was a family of specially designed wood framing members. These new wood members were felt to be less costly and easier to assemble than the standard wood studs and joists currently used in residential construction. Well, a detailed analysis of the residential framing market convinced the company that the potential for their new framing concept was not good. Building codes and trade unions were two major obstacles.

About a year later, this same company came to me and announced that they had done some initial analysis that led them to the conclusion that they should be in the motor-home business. They requested us to analyze this type of business for them. Again the detailed information gathering and analysis work uncovered several factors that convinced the company that motor homes were not that desirable a business opportunity. The fuel crisis, which followed shortly thereafter, reconfirmed this decision; motor-home sales collapsed during the crisis, and several leading manufacturers went into bankruptcy.

The next time around, this company finally got what they were looking for. After more initial analysis work, they asked us to analyze the Canadian mining industry for them. It turned out that the fit was very good, so after an acquisition search, a Canadian company was purchased. One slight hitch developed, however. It seems that the Canadian company owned a subsidiary that was in the lumber business in northern Wisconsin, and this subsidiary was purchased along with the mining company in a package deal. So the big company that had decided about three years earlier not to enter the building products area was in it after all. Not only were they in it, but they were in the wood framing business. This was the specific product area they had rejected earlier. So you see, even the big companies have trouble selecting a business, and when they do, it can turn out to be more than they bargained for.

YOUR DECISION

It's quite common, as pointed out in the above examples, for individuals looking for a small business opportunity and for large companies looking for diversification to decide against their initial business selections. A friend of mine, who also is a management consultant, took it to the extreme. He spent all his spare time during a two-year period analyzing different types of businesses and specific business opportunities. Finally, all the effort and patience paid off. He and his wife bought a franchise for a maternity fashion boutique. The business is doing well and they're both very happy. He has since gone on to start a trucking company with his brother, while his wife runs the boutique.

I'm not suggesting that you spend two years analyzing businesses. The example I just sited was an extreme case. But it may at least be worth your while to take a look at your second-ranking business type. After all, the grass always appears to be greener on the other side. And, in fact, it may be greener. But you'll never know unless you spend the time to take a look.

When you reach the point where you're ready to make a commitment to a specific business type, whether it be your initial selection, your second-ranking selection, or any other business type, there is a simple decision rule to guide you. If, for a specific business type, you can answer yes to all three of the following questions, you're ready to make a commitment:

1. Does the business satisfy most of the wants and desires (that is, business selection criteria) I'm seeking in a business?

2. Do I have, or can I develop (or hire), the attributes and capabilities that are required for success in this business?

3. Is the current condition and outlook for this business type good?

You probably recall that these are the three questions that you used in the last chapter to put the information you collected into categories, so for each business type you've analyzed you have three questions and three corresponding sets of information. The information in each category should allow you to answer yes or no to each corresponding question.

If you can answer yes to all three questions, you're in great shape. But even after looking at three or four businesses, the best you may be able to come up with is two yeses and a maybe. What then? At this point it boils down to one thing. Call it a "feeling," call it "intuition," or even call it a "hunch." If you've got a positive feeling about one of the business types, based on all the people you've talked to and based on all the information you've gathered, then I say that the one "maybe" is probably very close to being your third yes. And I say you're ready to commit to a business type.

On the other hand, if there are still some serious doubts in your mind about each type of business you've analyzed, it may be best to postpone your decision to commit to a business. Possibly you should visit more business owners and discuss your doubts with them, openly and freely. Because of their intimate knowledge of the business, they will probably be able to either confirm or dispel your reservations. If not, you really have only two choices. One is to make a commitment, despite your doubts. The other choice is to gather information and analyze another new business type. The decision must be yours. But remember, there is probably no perfect business. None will suit you exactly right; you're going to have to make some compromises. But if the choice is between remaining an unhappy and frustrated employee, or making a few compromises so you can be in your own business, then I think you'll be much happier in the long run if you make the compromises.

When you've made your commitment, you're halfway home. You've finished step one of the business selection process. Congratulations! Now you can go right on to Part III, where you'll see how to go about selecting your specific business opportunity.

PART

III
SELECTING YOUR SPECIFIC OPPORTUNITY

9

HOW THE GIANT
CORPORATIONS DO IT

*A business man's judgment is no
better than his information.*

ROBERT PATTERSON LAMONT

This is the first of six chapters that will illustrate in detail the best approach to selecting your specific small business opportunity. It's the same approach used by giant corporations. In this chapter you'll see how large corporations go about spending millions of dollars each year analyzing and selecting acquisitions, new products, and new business concepts. In the next chapter you'll see how you can apply these same "big business techniques" to your selection. And believe me, there's nothing difficult or complicated about it. It's nothing you can't do yourself with some time and effort and very little expense.

In three chapters of Part III, you'll see how to apply business research and analysis techniques to specific small business entry situations. First, the approach to selecting a franchise opportunity is detailed, and the important considerations for each type of franchise are examined. Next, you'll see how to select a start-up opportunity. An important distinction is drawn in this chapter between the two basic types of small business start-up situations. Finally, in the last chapter of Part III, you'll see how to select an ongoing business. Although you won't have a specific interest in all three methods of entering a small business, you will probably be interested in at least two of the three. If, for example, your business type selection is a fast-food franchise, you should consider entering through a new franchise or through the purchase of an ongoing franchise. Or if your business type selection is a machine shop, or a retailing operation, you should consider entering through both the start-up method and through the purchase of an ongoing business.

Before examining the approach used by giant companies in selecting specific business opportunities, some background information on their philosophy and motives will be helpful. Since the people in large companies who make decisions about acquisitions and new products generally do not get directly involved in the operation of new ventures, the business selection criteria for a large company is much different than that of an individual looking for a small business. For instance, you and I are interested in such things as personal achievement goals, status, and impacts on our life-style. Big business generally is interested only in three things. The first and foremost consideration is profit, or "bottom-line results" as it is called. The other two considerations of most big businesses are growth potential and large market-size potential. Most large companies will get involved in any business that meets their requirements in these three areas. For example, the consulting firm I am associated with has done acquisition studies for a large food company in such diverse product categories as travel trailers, luggage, kitchen cabinets, and stereo equipment.

However, there are some large companies that have one additional requirement. It's called "synergism" in the business community. What it means is that a company will add new businesses or products only in areas that are related to the mainstream business activity. In other words, a food company following this policy would diversify only into food-related businesses. A currently popular acquisition opportunity for large food companies who want to expand only into related businesses is restaurant chains.

The fact that most big companies are willing, and in fact do, expand into any large, growing, and profitable business area creates a need on their part for a great deal of information. Since, going back to the earlier example, a food company has no knowledge or experience in the luggage business, it must obtain this information in order to make a sound acquisition or new-product decision. So, you see, the large, sophisticated company is no better off than you are. You both need to implement business research and analysis techniques in order to wisely select a specific business opportunity.

Large companies basically have two methods by which to enter a new business area. Entry can be accomplished either through what is commonly called "internal development" or through acquisition of an already existing company. Internal development is generally a time-consuming process because of the necessity to complete the product research and development cycle, to purchase and install production facilities and equipment, and to build up marketing skills. Typically, internal development is used to enter a new-product area only if the new product is similar to existing product lines. Acquisition, the second method of entry, is used to diversify into totally foreign product areas. What this all says is that in big business, the less familiar a company is with a diversification opportunity, the more likely it is to buy an ongoing business.

But the reasoning behind this practice does not carry over into your decision on how best to enter a small business. First, the time-consuming nature of starting "from scratch" is not a major concern for most small businesses. Also, starting from scratch provides a great learning experience. Second, when a small business is purchased, say a clothing store, the single most important asset, the previous owner, typically walks out the door forever as soon as the deal is closed. So don't make the erroneous judgment that, just because the big guys are always buying up businesses, you are best served by doing the same thing. There are times when buying an ongoing small business is the best way, but this is not always true.

THE BIG BUSINESS APPROACH TO SELECTING A SPECIFIC BUSINESS OPPORTUNITY

Large companies typically have an internal staff whose primary purpose is associated with expansion of the business. In some companies this staff is called the market planning department. In others it is called corporate planning. And some companies have both, with the market planning department responsible for expansion of existing product lines and corporate planning responsible for new business opportunities. The people in these functions, regardless of the name of the group, are, among other things, constantly monitoring business trends and looking for high-growth opportunities. Potential new areas are screened against the company's profit, growth, and market-potential criteria.

Once an attractive business type has been identified, a rough screening of the major competitors is completed. The purpose of this screening is to identify, primarily from published information, the profitability, ownership status (e.g., public, private, division of another corporation), and product lines of each competitor. A likely acquisition candidate may then be identified.

This is the rational way in which acquisition candidates are identified. There are millions of irrational ways. They range from "hints" dropped by the financial community all the way to cocktail-party gossip. I recall one instance where the president of a major conglomerate found out that XYZ Company was for sale when he stopped for a drink in a hotel bar in New York. He just happened to bump into an old college classmate who was now the vice-president of XYZ. It didn't take long for the discussion to get around to a possible acquisition.

No matter how it happens, once an acquisition candidate is identified, three considerations are usually involved in a purchase decision: market, financial, and legal. Market considerations concern the current competitive position and outlook of the acquisition candidate. If the results are positive, then financial considerations (e.g., purchase price, audits) and legal considerations (e.g., restraint of trade, licenses) are analyzed. In most situations, market considerations are the key, as they should be. A company may be available at a bargain-basement price and the merger may have no serious legal problems, but if this company is a third-rate competitor and is losing market share, who'd want to buy it. Market considerations are also of preeminent importance in small business situations.

Before we get into the methods that are used by big business to analyze market considerations, some discussion of the nature of market considerations is appropriate. It's difficult to state concisely a definition or meaning of the term *market considerations*. It encompasses a broad range of factors. The most visible market considerations are market share and growth potential. Other important market considerations are product quality, price competitiveness, delivery and service reputation, and the image a company has with its current and past customers.

The study of market considerations is usually called a market analysis. A market analysis of an acquisition candidate can be done in one of two ways. It can be performed by the marketing planning or corporate planning staff of the acquiring company, or it can be done by an independent management consulting firm. It's my opinion that many times consultants do a better job. I can't help but think of two clients of the consulting firm I'm associated with. Both are multibillion-dollar conglomerates who are always actively acquiring companies. But the similarity ends there. One of the companies has us do the market analysis and the other one does its own analysis. You may wonder why the company that does its own market analysis is considered a client. It's because they are. We generally are asked to find out why the acquisition they made two years ago is in trouble. That's how I know they do an ineffective job of market analysis!

Do management consultants have an expertise that allows them to do something that companies themselves can't do? Or that you can't do? Do they have special knowledge or experience in an industry that allows them to pass judgment on an acquisition candidate? The answer to all these questions is *no*. You may recall that earlier I said that the consulting firm I'm with did kitchen-cabinet, travel-trailer, stereo-equipment, and luggage market analysis for one diversified company. Well, I can guarantee you, when each of these studies began, no one on our staff knew anymore than you do about these products.

Why, then, do large companies hire consulting firms to do market analysis work? There are many reasons, but the main ones are associated with availability of manpower, timing, and the desire of the company to protect their anonymity. Consulting firms have a readily available pool of manpower, can complete the work in a relatively short period of time because full effort can be devoted to it, and by using a consulting firm no one knows "who's really asking the questions." Management consultants have one other asset: the wherewithal to gather facts and opinions from a wide variety of sources and make some sense out of them. Fortunately, this skill is not possessed exclusively by consultants. Anyone with motivation and average intelligence can gather facts and opinions and make some sense out of them. You've already started doing it in your discussions with small business owners, and you'll learn everything else you'll need to know about it in the next five chapters of this book.

Hiring of a management consulting firm to do a market analysis study of an acquisition candidate begins with a preliminary meeting between the two. Specific details of the particular situation are discussed, and the major questions to be answered are agreed upon. Following this meeting, the consulting company writes a proposal to the acquiring company. This proposal is in fact a concise description of the work to be done during the market analysis. It's a work plan. This work plan is important to us because it describes each of the major steps in a market analysis study. It includes the objective of the study, the major information required, and the questions to be answered. It also covers methodology to be used, the time required to complete the work, and finally, the approximate cost.

The objectives of the study are generally stated in fairly broad terms, such as "to determine the desirability of acquiring the ABC Company." Information and questions to be answered almost always include:

- What is the current size of the market? How is it segmented by product type? What share does each leading company command?

- What has been the industry's past growth rate? What factors will affect future growth?

- What growth rate can ABC Company expect to attain in the next five-year period? Why?

- Where are ABC's products positioned in the market? Is this a favorable position from a growth and gross margin viewpoint?

- Are ABC Company's products competitively priced? What has been the price trend in the industry?

- What is the image of the ABC Company with its customers, its competitors, and its suppliers? Is the company considered a leader or follower? Why?

- How does the ABC Company stack up in the areas of service and delivery? Has this reputation changed in the recent past? Why?

The methodology section of the proposal is probably the most important area for you to understand, because you can apply exactly the same methodology to your selection. Typically, the methodology involved in a market analysis study concentrates on getting original data from as many different types of sources as possible. You're already familiar with three of them: trade associations, publications, and competitors. *Competitors* is the term used to refer to companies in the same business as the acquisition candidate. We called them "small business owners" in Chapter 7. Somehow, small business owner sounds less ominous than competitor. Other types of sources include suppliers, customers, sales agents, distributors, and even ex-employees of the acquisition candidate.

The philosophy associated with multiple-type sources is very important, yet quite simple. It provides the opportunity to collect different kinds of information from different types of sources; it allows the consultant to view the company from all perspectives; it provides for a method of cross-checking information; and it ensures that a complete analysis has been done. In the next chapter you'll see how to apply this approach to selecting your specific small business opportunity.

Market analysis studies associated with an acquisition are usually completed in six to ten weeks. This is somewhat shorter than the typical consulting assignment because of the urgency that's usually associated with making the purchase decision. But urgency is one thing, and panic is something else altogether. One of our clients, who usually does their own market analysis work, procrastinated too long on one acquisition. Six days before their option to buy was to expire, they called us up in sheer panic and begged us to do a "best-efforts" analysis. We did. The acquisition was consummated, and luckily for everybody, it turned out to be a good purchase. The length of time your selection analysis takes will obviously depend on the time you're able to donate to it. But don't count on anything less than two months if you want to do a thorough job.

Market analysis studies done by consulting firms are expensive. Large companies generally pay more for an acquisition-associated market analysis than it costs to start or buy a small business. Professional fees generally range from $15,000 to $60,000. Travel and other expenses add another 20 to 30 percent to the cost. This is why most small business owners can't afford to use management consultants, especially when they're quite able to accomplish the same objective, at very low cost, by doing the work themselves.

Following the acceptance of the consulting firm's proposal, another meeting usually is held between the firm and the acquiring company. Although this meeting is designed to review all facets of the upcoming study, it often boils down to a detailed discussion of the questions to be asked during the fieldwork phase of the study. Questions not originally included in the proposal are added at this time. In the next major step of the study, the consulting firm gathers together and categorizes the questions, using them to develop interview guides. Usually a different interview guide is used for each different type of source. Customer sources, for example, would have a different guide than distributor sources. The reason for this is that each source type has a different group of questions that they can respond to accurately, since each source type has a different relationship to the acquisition candidate.

At about the same time the interview guides are being prepared, several members of the consulting firm usually visit the headquarters of the acquisition candidate. The purpose of this visit is for the consulting firm to become as familiar as possible with the operations of the candidate's business. Products, marketing approaches, and distribution methods are discussed along with many other issues. Catalogs, price sheets, financial statements, and any other relevant information is gathered. This is an important step, because as you'll see later on, at this phase of the market analysis a direct parallel exists between big business and small business approaches.

The consulting firm is now ready to begin the most important phase of the market analysis. It's called "fieldwork" because it involves getting out in the marketplace and gathering all the necessary facts and opinions. Basically it involves asking all the questions on the interview guides to a large number of the right people. Generally, personal visits are made with the acquisition candidate's suppliers, distributors, sales agents, customers, and competitors. You remember the "rule" about always asking the easy questions first in a visit with a small business owner. Well, there is a similar rule concerning the order of approaching different types of sources. It is: Always try to do the easier (meaning the sources most likely to be cooperative) visits first and always save the competitors until last. Typical easy sources are trade associations, publishers, and customers of the acquisition candidate. The competitors are saved until last for two reasons. First, they are the single most important source of information. Second, they are the most likely to be uncooperative, so the ability to "trade" previously gathered information may be essential to encourage their participation in the fieldwork. The implications of this rule on small business market analysis will be discussed further in the next chapter.

Earlier I mentioned that one of the reasons large companies hire consulting firms to do market analysis studies is to protect their anonymity. That is, the consulting firm usually will not disclose, to any of the sources, the client who is paying for the market analysis. Another important consideration that is never disclosed during an acquisition-related market analysis study is the purpose of the study. This might sound somewhat baffling. You might be saying, "How can you go out and ask all these specific questions about the ABC Company without disclosing, or having people figure out, that you're analyzing the ABC Company?" Well, it's not done by misrepresenting the purpose of the visit. It's done by avoiding the purpose or by camouflaging it. Typically, the purpose of the study is described in such vague terms as, "We're doing a marketing study for a company who has an interest in the yo-yo market or the widget market." During visits with people, the ABC Company is camouflaged by also asking about two or three other leading companies in the same business. There are times while doing small business fieldwork when you may want to camouflage your purpose, so keep these techniques in mind.

Following completion of the fieldwork, all the information that has been gathered is analyzed and a report is prepared. Although a great deal of effort is usually involved in this final phase, very little is really relevant to the small business situation. The management consulting firm spends most of this phase organizing material and writing a report so that it will be easily understood by people (the client) who were not directly involved in the study itself—people who need a clearly written, straightforward presentation of findings and conclusions. Fortunately, you don't have to spend time on such an effort. Since you will be your own client, and since you did all the work, you'll be intimately familiar with the findings and be able to draw conclusions without an elaborate report.

A BIG COMPANY MARKET ANALYSIS

Several years ago a client of ours came to the consulting firm I'm associated with and said that they were considering the acquisition of a smallish automotive accessories supplier. The client company was a billion-dollar-plus supplier of components to the Big Three auto makers. The acquisition candidate was about a $10-million-dollar company that was actually composed of four businesses. Each did approximately $2 to $3 million in sales. Three of the businesses were in the automotive products manufacturing area. One sold radiator cores to auto repair shops. Another made truck radiators, and the third made engine heaters (these are used in Canada and states such as Minnesota and North Dakota to assist in cold-weather starting by keeping the engine warm when the car is parked overnight). The fourth business activity was in the building products area.

This acquisition example is important to us for several reasons. First, since each of the businesses of the acquisition candidate made only $2 million to $3 million, this study really concerns four separate small business market analysis studies. Second, since some of the products in this acquisition study are sold through distributors and retailers, this example demonstrates a methodology that is applicable not only to the purchase of a manufacturing company, but also to the purchase of a distributor, and to some extent, the purchase of a retailer. Finally, this particular example will demonstrate that even big-city management consultants sometimes have trouble with competitive interviews, and that big corporation presidents lose interest during long afternoon meetings, just like everybody else.

At one of the initial meetings with the client company, several important decisions were made. The building product business actually accounted for less than a quarter of the candidate's sales revenue and was in an altogether different end market (residential construction) from the automotive-related businesses. Therefore it was decided, because of time constraints, to not analyze this area. It was also decided to look at the three automotive product areas as three separate market analysis studies. This was done because each had separate production facilities, sales forces, and distribution channels, and different customers.

As mentioned earlier, the first automotive-related business produced radiator cores. A radiator core is the finned portion that you think of when you picture a car radiator. It is typically soldered between two tanks. The core and the two tanks make up a radiator assembly. The radiator core is used by radiator repair shops to repair clogged radiators or those damaged in auto accidents. Specialized machines are used by core manufacturers to cheaply assemble the wide variety of cores required. Seven different source types were used to gather and cross-check information. These seven sources and the number of meetings completed with each source during the course of the study are shown below:

Source	Number completed
Trade associations	1
Publications	2
Specialized machinery suppliers	2
Copper-strip suppliers	3
Radiator-core distributors	5
Radiator repair shops	10
Competitors (core manufacturers)	4
Total	27

Surprisingly, the most difficult meetings were those with the radiator repair shops—not because the owners were uncooperative, but because they often didn't have a quiet place to sit down and talk. It seems that most of them operated from a small desk or office adjoining the shop area. Since, in this analysis, the shop owners were customers (less important) and not competitors (most important) of the acquisition candidate, it wasn't deemed necessary to "get them away" from their business for lunch or a dinner meeting.

There was one less source type in the truck-radiator market analysis, since the marketing channel is direct from the radiator manufacturers to the final customer (truck manufacturers). No intermediate distributor is used. In this market analysis the following types and number of sources were contacted:

Source	Number completed
Trade associations	1
Publications	3
Copper-strip suppliers	3
Fastener and fitting suppliers	2
Truck manufacturers	12
Competitors (radiator manufacturers)	5
Total	26

In this analysis, as was the case in the radiator-core market analysis, the number of meetings for the competitors represents coverage of *all* the major competitors. It's generally a good idea in any market analysis to do all, or most all, of the competitors. Earlier I mentioned that this example demonstrated that sometimes management consultants have trouble completing competitive interviews. Well, it was in this portion of the study when it happened to me. I had made an appointment to see the marketing manager of a major competitor by simply explaining on the phone "that I was doing a market study in the truck-radiator area." I was even nice enough to offer him some informal "feedback" of information after the study was completed. He sounded a little apprehensive when I called but no more than many people do. Yet when I showed up at his office the morning of my appointment, he was as cold as ice and not the least bit cooperative. He wanted to know who the study was being done for and why it was being done. I couldn't tell him. He insisted on knowing, so I had no choice but to terminate the meeting. Luckily you won't have the same problem, because who you're working for (yourself) and your purpose will probably not be a secret, in most cases.

The last product category to be analyzed in this acquisition study was engine heaters. Engine heaters are sold through three distinct distribution channels. The most direct channel is from the heater manufacturers to the new-car manufacturers. The second channel is through the traditional automotive-parts distribution levels, which include the warehouse distributor, the jobber, the auto parts dealer, and sometimes the service station. The final major channel of distribution is direct to mass merchandisers such as Sears. In order to thoroughly analyze the competitive position and future potential of the acquisition candidate's products, it was necessary to gather information from all three channels. The different sources and the number of meetings completed with each source during the course of the analysis are shown on the following page.

The engine-heater manufacturers' meetings were interesting because the size of the companies spanned the entire spectrum. The largest manufacturer was a Fortune-100 company, and the small-

Source	Number completed
Trade associations	0
Publications	4
Heating-element suppliers	2
Auto manufacturers	4
Warehouse distributors	8
Jobbers	6
Auto parts dealers	6
Mass retailing	5
Competitors (engine-heater manufacturers)	5
Total	40

est company was "something else." I'll never forget the meeting I had with the owner of this company. He was the entrepreneurial inventor type who had such an overdeveloped sense of secrecy that he wouldn't meet with me in his place of business. Although he wasn't a big factor in the market, his company had just introduced a new concept in engine heaters, and I was most interested in discussing it with him. When I called to make an appointment, he suggested I meet him at his apartment at four o'clock in the afternoon.

I announced my arrival on the building intercom system, and he said, "I'll be right down." I didn't know what he was up to until he came down, shook hands, and said, "I've got some highly confidential drawings upstairs, so why don't we just ride around and talk." He insisted on driving. We meandered through the streets for one and a half hours, with me asking questions and taking notes and him answering questions and doing his best to drive. The meeting was extremely productive, but I was very relieved when it was over. I now consider myself an expert at writing in a moving car.

There is an important factor to note in the methodologies of the three separate market analysis studies. Although the results of each study were of equal importance, more than a fair share of the meetings were conducted in the engine-heater analysis, as indicated on the following page. This resulted from a need to

Market analysis	Number of meetings
Radiator cores	27
Truck radiators	26
Engine heaters	40

be complete and thorough. As mentioned earlier, engine heaters are marketed through three separate distribution channels. Each channel was significant, so the key sources in each channel had to be contacted. This situation also carries over into the small business area. That is, the number of contacts necessary to thoroughly complete the analysis of a specific small business opportunity is not necessarily related to the size of the business. It is more dependent on the nature of the business, the diversity of distribution channels, the number of significant competitors, and other considerations associated with the specific situation.

Following completion of fieldwork for each of the three separate studies, the analysis and report writing was begun. The facts and opinions demonstrated overwhelmingly that the acquisition candidate was indeed an attractive find. Profitability was expected to continue at high levels. The company was found to be a leader in each market in which it competed. And finally, all three product lines had significant growth potential and each had an apparent opportunity for product-line expansion. Based on these major findings, the report concluded with a recommendation to acquire.

A meeting to present the results of the acquisition study was scheduled to take place exactly ten weeks after the program was begun. It took place at the client's headquarters on a Friday afternoon. A board of directors meeting was held that same morning, followed by an appropriate luncheon. Maybe it was the luncheon that took its toll on the president. He had his jacket off and his tie loosened soon after the acquisition meeting began, and guess what happened just as the presentation was reaching its climax. The president and chief executive officer of this billion-dollar company dozed off. His head bobbed, his eyes closed, and he was out. His senior vice-president "accidentally" nudged him back to consciousness just as we stated our recommendation! He swallowed it hook, line, and sinker! The acquisition was announced in the financial press the following week. This company continues to be a good client of ours, and to this day, whenever I see the president or hear someone mention his name, I see an image of a very sleepy man fighting to keep his eyes open. I should end the commentary by saying, in all fairness, that this man has done an excellent job of leading his company.

OBJECTIVITY

Big companies have one thing going for them that is difficult, in many cases, for a person entering a small business to match. These companies can usually make fairly objective decisions concerning acquisitions and new-product introduction. Most big business decisions that I've been associated with were made in an impartial manner, in the absence of any noticeable emotional involvement.

I'm not saying that there aren't managers working with every large company who aren't promoting or advocating a particular action. They're always there, because a job advancement may be involved. Or, on the other hand, their job may be at stake. But usually, major decisions are not made by people who will be directly benefited or hurt by them. These kinds of decisions are made by top-level management, whose job security depends mainly on the overall success of the entire corporation. Because of this, top-level management usually makes very calculating, unemotional acquisition and new-business-venture decisions.

I remember a study our consulting firm carried out several years ago for a large rubber company. One of its divisions was involved in the production and marketing of specialized vinyl products. The division was not doing well, so the rubber-company management asked for our opinion. Specifically, they wanted the answers to two questions: Should we stay in the specialized vinyl products business or get out? And, if we stay, what should we do to make it profitable? For many of the people in the division, their jobs and security could be riding on the answers. Obviously these people were not in a position to make objective decisions. They wanted to stay in the business and expand it, and they had the "facts" to demonstrate that this was the only intelligent course of action. Well, I'm sorry to say, the information and opinions we gathered in our study strongly suggested that the only wise course for the rubber company to take was to get out of the business. This group of specialized vinyl products competed in a saturated, stagnant, highly price-conscious market. None of the other competitors were making any money either. We had no choice but to make a recommendation that was consistent with our findings. Top-level management accepted our conclusion and initiated action to phase out the vinyl products division. This is just one example of difficult, yet objective, decisions that are made by big companies every day.

Once in a while, large companies do make the mistake of becoming emotionally involved in acquisition and business-venture decisions. Just recently, we did an acquisition analysis for a regular client of ours. In the past they had always been very objective. But not this time. The acquisition candidate was in the home stereo products area. The group vice-president of our client company "grew up" in the same business. He prided himself on his knowledge of stereo equipment, and he apparently wanted nothing more than to make the acquisition so he could get back into it. This was almost understandable, but for some mysterious reason the manager of acquisitions also became emotionally involved. These two people reached the point where they suggested that we "carefully phrase any negative-sounding findings" when presenting our results to the president and board chairman. "If you don't, you could make things sound a lot worse than they really are," explained the vice-president. To make matters more difficult, our findings were neither black nor white; they were gray. However, because of their predisposition, the two men saw everything as just slightly off pure white. I suspect that the acquisition may turn out to be a disaster, but it's still too early to tell.

The message from all this is straightforward. Try to remain objective when making your small business selection decision. I know that's easier said than done, because it's even hard to be objective when buying a house or a new car. It's surely more difficult when selecting a small business. You might not be able to remain emotionally uninvolved throughout the entire process, but try to hold out as long as possible, because falling in love too soon will cloud your good judgment.

CHAPTER

10

HOW YOU CAN UTILIZE BUSINESS ANALYSIS TO SELECT A SPECIFIC BUSINESS OPPORTUNITY

Have patience. All things are
difficult before they become easy.
SAADI

In the last chapter we saw how the corporate giants go about selecting specific business opportunities. It's not magical, or even terribly sophisticated, is it? In this chapter you'll see how to take the big business approach and apply it to any specific small business opportunity. The basic techniques and common denominators for all small business research and analysis are presented. And then in the three following chapters you'll see how to apply these techniques to a franchise opportunity, an ongoing business, and finally to a start-up opportunity.

All the techniques detailed in these four chapters are designed to be used on a specific small business opportunity. By specific I mean a McDonald's franchise in Toledo or a hobby shop in a new shopping center in Dearborn, Michigan. Just as in the last chapter, the large-company market analysis studies were aimed at a specific acquisition candidate or a specific new product. I'm emphasizing this point now because you may be wondering how you're going to bridge the gap that appears to exist between your business type selection and the many specific opportunities. For example, say the business type that you're committed to is a fast-food franchise. How do you go from a fast-food franchise to a

McDonald's franchise in Toledo? Well, it's really quite easy. But it depends a lot on the type of business you're committed to. It's not the same for a fast-food franchise and for an ongoing manufacturing business. For this reason, the discussion of the transition from a business type to specific opportunities is covered for each particular case in the three chapters that follow.

When you get further into this chapter, you may notice some similarities between the information gathering you did to confirm your business type selection and the market analysis techniques used to analyze a specific small business opportunity. The approaches are similar. Both rely on an organized system of gathering information and analyzing it. But there is a great deal of difference too. The information gathering you did earlier was designed for a specific, limited purpose, while the market analysis techniques used to analyze a specific small business opportunity are much more comprehensive. Because of the similarities, your previous information-gathering experience will be very helpful in pursuing the goal of selecting the specific small business opportunity that's right for you.

Each section of this chapter is devoted to a major step in the specific small business analysis process. Let's get to the first step.

STATE YOUR OBJECTIVES CLEARLY AND CONCISELY

To some people, this may seem like a trivial way to begin, but it really isn't. Stating your objectives clearly and concisely is important because it forces you to focus your attention on the purpose of the analysis.

Webster defines the word *objective* as "something toward which effort is directed; an end or an aim of action." What is the something toward which your effort is directed? What is your end or your aim? It's important to try to state your objective as simply as possible. If you can do it in one sentence, that's great. Here are a few examples that may be helpful:

- My objective is to analyze the fast-food franchises that are available and to select the one that offers the best opportunity.

- My objective is to buy a small manufacturing business. I'll use this base to support myself and to expand into other products.

- My objective is to start an antique shop. I need to find out the best way of going about it.

Be sure to write your objective down and keep it handy. You may find it helpful to look back at it from time to time, especially if you feel you're bogged down or drifting during the course of your analysis.

LAY OUT A WORK PLAN

There are many people who start their workday by making a list of things that they expect to (or must) get done that day. Then they methodically cross off each item as it is completed. I must admit I'm a list maker and that I really believe in the merits of these lists. They help me avoid forgetting important things that must be done. They allow me to keep track of my progress as the day goes on. And I get great satisfaction out of crossing off the last item on the list. Somehow it makes me feel that I've done a good day's work.

But the single most important asset of my list of things to do is that it gets me organized. It points me in the right direction and keeps me on track. That's what a work plan will do for you. A work plan is nothing more than a list of things to do—not in one day, but during your analysis of specific small business opportunities.

Fortunately, there is a basic work plan that is good for almost all small business types and situations, and it's the same one used in most big business market analysis studies. We went through most of the plan in some detail in the last chapter when discussing the steps that are included in a typical management consulting firm's acquisition analysis proposal. To these steps we must add special market research techniques, financial analysis, and legal analysis:

1. Develop a master list of questions to be answered.

2. Develop a list of sources of information.

3. Write the interview guides.

4. Gather secondary-source information.

5. Do the fieldwork:

    Personal meetings

    Telephone

6. Use specialized market research techniques.

7. Make market analysis and conclusions.

8. Do financial analysis.

9. Do legal analysis.

10. Make decision.

Earlier I said that this work plan is good for almost all small business types and situations. You can personalize it to your specific requirements just by filling in some details. For example, in step two you might note the different types of sources. In step three you may want to indicate the specific interview guides that are to be prepared. And in step five you could elaborate more specifically on the nature and form of the contacts you expect to make.

In the next section we're going to discuss the importance of making a time schedule for completing each step of the work plan. Then in the remaining sections of this chapter, you'll see how to accomplish each step of the work plan.

SET UP A TIME SCHEDULE

There are no time clocks, no bosses, no one to tell you what to do or when to do it in a small business. When a bookkeeper comes to work and doesn't feel like keeping the books that day, he keeps them anyway because he knows that the boss will be angry or fire him if he is caught sitting around reading a magazine. As a result the work gets done. The person who is looking for a small business opportunity, however, is his or her own boss, and too often the work may not get done. This complete lack of time clocks and bosses, in addition to being one of the most wonderful aspects of being your own boss, can also be its biggest headache.

Through the years, people have invented a multitude of reasons and excuses to avoid starting their own businesses. One of the best excuses is associated with a lack of time. It goes something like: "I just don't have the time with the pressures of my job, the family, and all the other things I have to do. When am I going to find the time to do all the things that I know have to be done to get a business going." Sure we're all busy, but as the old saying goes, "Where there is a will, there is a way." If you've got the will, the best way to find the time to select your business opportunity is to set up a time schedule and promise to do your best to stick to it. You'll be constantly reminded that your schedule calls for completion of this or that by such and such a date. Then it's hoped you'll find the time to accomplish it. Maybe it will require missing your regular Saturday-morning tee-off time or a Friday-night card game, but won't it be worth it?

Remember the list I said I make each morning when I begin my work? Well, that list keeps me on schedule because completion of the items on the list is associated with a specific time period. Completion usually is scheduled for that very day. The same is true for the items on a time schedule, except that the time of completion will be so many weeks from now, instead of today.

Your time schedule should be directly tied into the work plan that was described earlier. A good schedule can be developed by trying to accurately estimate how long it will take to complete each step of the work plan. These "blocks of time" can then be converted into scheduled completion dates for each step of the work plan by using a calendar.

Scheduled completion dates will depend a great deal on the type of business in which you are selecting your specific opportunity. These dates will also depend on whether you're analyzing a franchise opportunity, a start-up opportunity, or an ongoing business. However, I can give you some rough guidelines for the time required to complete each step of a typical work plan. You can modify them, if necessary, based on your specific type of business, the amount of time you have available each week, and on the more specific information that will be presented in the next three chapters.

Work-plan step	Days required to complete
1. Master list of questions	1
2. Sources of information	2
3. Interview guides	1
4. Secondary-source information	3
5. Fieldwork	10–40
6. Specialized market research techniques	2–10
7. Market analysis and conclusions	3–6
8. Financial analysis	5–10
9. Legal analysis	5–10

YOUR MASTER LIST OF QUESTIONS

Remember the list of questions presented in Chapter 7? The list is called "Basic Questions for Business Owners," and it begins on page 77. Well, what we're trying to do now is a very similar, yet very different, kind of list. The similarity lies in the fact that here again we want to develop a list of questions to be used during information-gathering meetings with people. The primary difference lies in the questions themselves. The purpose of the earlier questions was to find out about the nature (that is, the owner's life-style, owner's work requirements, capabilities required for success, etc.) of one or two types of businesses. But now you want and need to be much more specific, because you're going to be thoroughly probing a particular business situation—the purchase of a restaurant franchise, starting a clothing store, or buying a beer distributorship in Peoria.

Your list of questions will obviously depend a great deal on the particular business opportunity you're evaluating. Guidance on developing your list for a franchise opportunity, for an ongoing business, and for a start-up opportunity is presented in Chapters 11, 12, and 13, respectively.

I was recently offered the opportunity to purchase a small company that manufactures medical instruments. Specifically, the company offered a complete line of biofeedback instruments. These instruments monitor body functions (brain waves) and are used in the treatment of tension headaches, anxiety, high blood pressure, and other maladies. The company was in its third year of operation; annual sales were approaching $100,000. To give you some idea of the type of questions that should be on your list, here are some of the questions I would put on my list were I to analyze this medical instrument company:

- What is the size of the market for this type of product? Who are the present and potential customers?

- When did these products first come on the market? How have sales grown since? What share of the total potential market has been tapped as of now? What is the outlook for the growth of the biofeedback instrument market?

- Who are the competitors? What are their market shares? What products do they offer? Who are their major customers? Are the competitors profitable? What is their personal appraisal of the future of this business?

- What is the image of the company I'm investigating? Is their technology progressive and forward thinking? How is the product's reliability? Has it lived up to expectations? Has service been adequate? How does its image compare with that of the competitors?

- Is biofeedback equipment considered an ethical medical treatment product? Or do some people consider it a hoax? Why? Is this attitude changing?

- Are new applications likely in the future? In what areas? Does the company have the products and know-how to exploit these applications?

- How have company sales changed from year to year? How does this compare with competitors' sales increases? What is causing the increases (or decreases) in sales in this company and for its competitors?

- What kind of marketing programs are being used by the company I'm investigating and by its competitors? What sells the product? Technical features? Flexibility? Price?

- What is the company's credit reputation? How prompt are payments to suppliers?

These are only some of the important questions, but they do give an idea of the type of questions that should be on your master list.

DEVELOP A LIST OF SOURCES OF INFORMATION

We already know three sources of information. You used them to verify your business type selection. They are trade associations, publications, and business owners. You may recall that large companies refer to business-owner sources as competitors. This is probably the label we should use from now on, because business owners you're talking to could in fact, some day, be your competitors.

There is a simple rule to identify sources of information beyond the three that were just mentioned. Other sources of information can be found by looking for any people or organization that comes in contact with the business you're investigating. Possibilities include customers (and competitors' customers), distributors, manufacturers' representatives, ex-employees, suppliers, bankers, stockbrokers, landlords, and even people who operate nearby businesses.

In the biofeedback instrument manufacturing example, there are some very important sources of information.

- Applied Biofeedback Institute (Denver, Colo.)

- Biofeedback Research Society (Denver, Colo.)

- Institute for Living (Hartford, Conn.)

- *Biofeedback and Self-Control* (Aldine-Acherton, Inc., Chicago)

- *New Mind, New Body Biofeedback,* Harper & Row, 1974.

- Hospitals and clinics

- Psychiatrists, psychologists, and medical doctors

- Customers and noncustomers

- Competitors

- Electronic-component suppliers

- Ex-employees and the landlord

WRITING THE INTERVIEW GUIDES

Again, you're off to a flying start because you've already prepared an interview guide to use in your business-owner meeting. The guides that you'll need for this analysis can utilize the same format. Remember, the easy questions go first, and leave space below each question to note the answer and anything else of interest that's said during the meeting. There are two differences though. First, the questions are different. Second, you'll need a separate interview guide for each different source type.

Getting back to my biofeedback situation, if I were to investigate that business opportunity, I'd need one guide for competitors, one for customers, one for hospitals and clinics, one for suppliers, and maybe one for all the other miscellaneous sources. The reason I'd need different guides for different sources is that I'd have different questions for each type of source. For example, on the customer interview guide I would have such questions as, "Why did you purchase an XYZ Company biofeedback instrument?" and, "How did it compare with competitors' instruments in capabilities, features, price, delivery?" These questions would not be appropriate on a competitor or any other interview guide.

The easiest way to write your interview guides is to take as many sheets of paper as you have different sources of information. On the top of each sheet write the appropriate source. Now, using the master list of questions you prepared earlier, write on each sheet of paper, one to a line, all the questions from your master list that apply to that source. When this is finished, you're ready to put your questions in "easiest-question-first" order. This is best done one sheet at a time. Take your first sheet and put a number 1 in front of the easiest, least threatening question. Put a number 2 in front of the next easiest, and so on until each question has a number. Now you can just take out a fresh pad of paper and write each interview guide by putting a heading on top of page 1 (for instance, customer interview guide) and then write the questions in the order you numbered them. Be sure to leave space to write in responses. Take as many sheets as necessary to complete each guide.

You'll need copies of each guide. You can either use carbon paper or have a quick-print service make them for you.

GATHERING SECONDARY-SOURCE INFORMATION

By the time you reach this stage of your business selection process, you'll already be an expert at gathering secondary-source information. *Secondary-source information* is the term used to refer to printed information. Typical examples you are already familiar with are trade association reports and booklets, trade magazines, SBA publications, the *Small Business Reporter* (Bank of America), and newsletters. You should review and recontact these sources if you feel they can assist you in answering any of the questions on your master list.

There are also some additional sources of secondary information that could prove to be very helpful at this stage of your analysis. The *Reader's Guide to Periodical Literature* (at your local library) should be reviewed for relevant articles. You might find a personal profile of a business in the same area you're investigating, or you might run across an article that prognosticates about the future of such-and-such a business. A good source of statistical information is the U.S. Department of Commerce. I'd suggest a letter or call to the nearest office, requesting a list of their reports, many of which are issued on a monthly or quarterly basis. Other government agencies may also be helpful depending on your specific situation. If you're investigating any business that's related to automobiles, for example, the U.S. Department of Commerce and the Environmental Protection Agency (EPA) have reams of information.

There's another source of secondary information, but it's somewhat of a long shot. It's the investment and brokerage houses. Sometimes they publish special reports analyzing a company or an entire industry. I just recently saw one that was done on the Pillsbury Company (which owns Burger King). This report went into great detail on Burger King and its major competitors and could be very helpful if you were thinking of buying a Burger King franchise. Write a few firms and ask them if they know of, or have published themselves, any reports in the area you're investigating. You might strike gold.

If you're selecting an opportunity where location is important (store, restaurant, auto repair shop, dry cleaner, etc.), you should get whatever demographic and traffic information is available. Your local planning commission and chamber of commerce should be able to assist you. And finally, there's a secondary source which shows comparative financial statements for different types of businesses. It's called *Robert Morris Associates Annual Statement Studies* and is used by banks in making loan decisions. Your local bank may be willing to let you look at a copy. I'd suggest a call to a loan officer, explaining your purpose and introducing yourself.

DOING THE PERSONAL FIELDWORK

It's time to put your interview guides to work. As was mentioned earlier, personal meetings are the best way to gather information. I'd suggest that you make every effort to do much of your fieldwork in person. The special situations where telephone calls can be substituted for personal visits are discussed in the next section.

In the consulting trade, fieldwork is typically referred to as interviewing, as in the comment, "On this program we're doing thirty customer, ten distributor and about six competitor interviews." I've been trying to minimize the use of the word *interview* for two reasons. First, I'm afraid it might make some of you feel uncomfortable. It is an ominous word, since most of our exposure to interviews is related to journalists' "interviewing" celebrities or politicians. Second, the use of the word *interview* as in "I'm evaluating the Kenny and Bruce fast-food restaurant franchise, and I know you operate two units so I'd like to stop in and interview you" will probably make most people feel very uncomfortable. So don't even use the word *interview* when talking to a source.

The interviews you'll do will be much different from the stereotype of the journalistic interview. As was recommended in your small-business-owner meetings, you should strive for an informal, friendly discussion, not a question-and-answer session. The only essentials of your "interviews" are that you must weave your questions into the discussion and that you'll want to take notes. The best way to get your questions in is to maintain control of the discussion. If your source drifts off to some fringe topic, bring the person back with your next question by saying something like, "Earlier you said . . . , could you expand on that by telling me about . . . [your next question] . . . ," and if the person's really drifting, it may actually be necessary to interrupt to interject this type of comment and question.

Some people are tempted to use a tape recorder for personal interviews. This approach usually creates more problems than it's worth. It may make your contacts feel very ill at ease. It also will require you to replay the entire interview at some later date in order to "sift out" the good information. If you record twenty 1-hour meetings, you'll have to listen to twenty hours of tape. Of course, if a tape recorder is used, it is never concealed. Hidden tape recorders are best left to undercover agents and politicians.

One last comment on personal fieldwork. Don't limit yourself to the questions on your interview guide. Ask any questions that seem important at the time. But don't forget to cover all the questions on your guide (always trying to ask the easy questions first). If a good question or two arises in a meeting, you should probably add these questions to the rest of the still-to-be-used copies of your guide. Then you'll be sure to remember these in future meetings.

DOING THE TELEPHONE FIELDWORK

Telephone fieldwork, or telephone interviewing, is not as effective as personal meetings. But it can, or must, be used in certain situations. The most obvious is when the travel distance is so great that you can't afford a personal visit. Then there are those situations where you only need a limited amount of information. For example, say you're planning to talk to a total of fifteen customers. After doing ten, you feel comfortable with most of the responses. You feel you only need additional answers to some of your questions. Phone calls to five customers might save you much time. One of the reasons telephone interviews are restricted to gathering limited information is the time element. Personal interviews will usually last an hour and maybe up to two hours. You just can't expect to keep someone on the phone nearly that long. The other serious deficiency of phone interviews is that the source replies are usually a little guarded because people are never quite sure who they're talking to.

Another situation where telephone interviews are appropriate is for less critical sources. A trade association, a publication, or some smaller customers may fall into this category. Telephone interviews should also be used for people who refuse to see you in person. After the refusal, you could say, "Well, how about if I just cover a few things now on the phone? It will only take a couple of minutes." The final purpose of phone interviews is for call-backs to ask a person you've visited (or telephoned) earlier a few additional specific questions or to ask for clarification of some issue.

There is one unfair advantage in telephone interviews. It's a woman's voice. In this business world that is saturated with males, a woman can work wonders on the telephone. Business men have been known to tell female interviewers things on the telephone they wouldn't tell their most trusted employees, or even their tax lawyers. If you're a woman, take advantage of your voice. This may sound sexist, but believe me, it works. And for you men, if you can talk a female friend or colleague into making a few calls for you, more power to you.

The basic approach to telephone interviews is the same as it is for personal interviewing. Briefly, the key guidelines are:

1. Ask easy questions first.

2. Avoid the use of the word *interview*.

3. Create a relaxed, informal discussion.

4. Weave your questions into the discussion.

5. Ask follow-up questions such as "Could you explain that further?"

6. Maintain control of the "discussion."

7. Take notes.

8. Add any new appropriate questions.

9. Ask all the questions on your guide—even the hard ones on the last page.

SPECIALIZED MARKET RESEARCH TECHNIQUES

There are two specialized market research techniques that may be important in selecting your particular small business opportunity. The first is site-selection analysis. The site or location is vital to the success of most retail businesses, whether they be restaurants, convenience food stores, dry cleaning shops, antique shops, or whatever. The second specialized market analysis technique is consumer market research. Consumer market research is the major market research tool of consumer product companies such as General Foods, Pillsbury, and Revlon. If your business opportunity involves manufacturing and marketing of a consumer product, you should probably develop some understanding of the simpler consumer market research approaches. Site selection and consumer market research are discussed separately in this section.

Site selection can be a very sophisticated and expensive undertaking. Shopping-center developers spend tens of thousands of dollars analyzing potential sites. And then they put out glowing, detailed reports that are used to attract potential tenants. Fortunately, you won't have to get involved in anything like this, because all you really need is common sense and some "digging" around.

The key to successful site selection is to understand, in the specific type of business you're starting (or buying), what makes for a successful site. You can do this by analyzing several successful existing business locations. Then all you have to do is simulate these characteristics when you're selecting a site (or buying an ongoing business). In fact, you may even be able to make a better selection by improving on other people's mistakes.

Basically, successful site location depends on four major factors:

1. Nature of the population in market area

2. Income in market area

3. The convenience and visibility of the site

4. Competition in the market area

These factors have varying degrees of importance depending on the nature of the business itself. You'll probably be able to relate to each better after you read the following two specific site-location examples:

1. Specialized automotive repair shops have very specific site-location requirements. Summarized below are the site-selection criteria for one of the major franchized auto transmission repair chains.

    A. *Market area:* Middle-class neighborhood with 25,000 to 75,000 car registrations.

    B. *Income:* Family income of $5000 to $16,000 a year. Avoid extremes.

    C. *Convenience and visibility:* Located on a main street (16,000 average daily traffic count). Two-way traffic (undivided). Speed limit not to exceed 45 mph. Corner location preferred. Freestanding sign to be visible at twenty-second visibility in both directions at posted speed limit. Building sign must be allowed to be painted on building (3 feet by 40 feet).

    D. *Competition:* No other similar outlets in area.

(Notice the emphasis on "middle income" in the first two criteria. This chain has found that extremes in income level are to be avoided. Higher-income car owners are likely to depend on the new car dealers for repairs or trade-in, rather than pay a $300 transmission repair bill. And lower-income car owners are felt to "junk them rather than repair them.")

2. The consulting firm I'm associated with did a site location study for a chain of carry-out fried-chicken restaurants in Chicago. The study was initiated because there was great variability in gross sales between stores that originally appeared to offer the same potential. Some stores had yearly sales of as low as $120,000 while others were doing almost $300,000 per year. An analysis of popula-

tion, income, convenience, visibility, and competition revealed that the best way to generate high annual gross sales was to locate stores in low-income black neighborhoods. Of course there were higher-income suburban locations that were doing well, but not as consistently as the inner-city low-income locations.

Now back to the four major factors. The best source of population data is the federal census. It is taken every ten years and gives not only total population, but also detailed breakdowns that are useful in many business situations. For most larger cities, census figures are further classified by sections within the city on the basis of specific population and economic characteristics. These sections are called census tracts. Specific neighborhoods can be viewed on census-tract maps from the U.S. Department of Commerce. When future development is a concern, the city or county planning commission may be able to help with copies of master plans or special reports. Population analysis should consider changes in total population over the past ten years, average family size, number of family units, current distribution and trends in distribution by age group, and the percentage of total population in your market area that are potential customers of your kind of business.

The ten-year census reports the income of 20 percent of the total population on a national, state, county, city, and census-tract basis. Other sources of income include the planning commission, employment offices, newspapers, building permits (especially in newly developed areas), and mortgage and loan companies. Income analysis should consider total spendable income in market area, average per capita income, average family income, and how much consumers typically spend for various classes of goods and services in your kind of market area.

Be sure to bring up the site-selection question in your discussions with business owners. Ask them how they chose their site. Probe for satisfactions and dissatisfactions. Find out what they think are the important factors related to selecting a site in their particular type of business. And don't forget to ask about the nature, proximity, and impact of local competition. On second thought, you might not even have to ask. Competition is usually one of business owners' favorite topics of conversation.

Consumer market research is the second specialized market research technique that could be useful in your business selection. Basically, consumer market research is a group of forecasting methods used to anticipate the success or failure of a new, untried consumer product before or soon after the product is put on the market. If your business type choice focuses on a new, untried consumer product, then consumer market research should be of interest to you. (There is, incidentally, another facet of consumer market research associated with established consumer products. But this area has little relevancy to your small business selection).

Consumer market research is a science and an industry in itself. Dozens of textbooks have been written on the subject. Most major consumer product companies have a full-time staff of consumer market research specialists. Millions of dollars are spent each year by many of these companies. One of the largest companies has an annual budget of $25 million for consumer market research alone. The *Market Research Green Book* lists hundreds of firms that specialize in assisting large companies to carry out their consumer market research projects.

Although the term *consumer market research* may not be familiar to you, you probably have been exposed to the heart of the process as a consumer. Most consumers have received questionnaires in the mail or telephone calls from market research firms. Perhaps you've even had someone come to your front door carrying a clipboard and asking questions about this or that product. These people are gathering consumer market research data. There is no basic reason why you or I can't collect similar data. Unfortunately, a problem develops at the next step of the process: analyzing and interpreting the data. This is where the big, sophisticated, computer-equipped companies have got it all over little guys like you and me. You see, what appears to be simple data is not; it is really a statistically relevant sample. This statistically relevant sample is then manipulated, massaged, and extrapolated using complex mathematical techniques, and an answer, usually right, but not always, pops out of the computer.

Luckily there is a way for us to accomplish much the same thing, without the relevant sample and the computer. Most new-product consumer market research is broken down into four phases. First there's concept screening, where numerous new-product concepts are ranked-based on their likelihood of success as seen by a consumer sample. Next, the winners are concept tested. This involves a more thorough and complete testing of a specific concept. If the concept still looks promising, limited production is authorized and a pretest market test is undertaken. This third phase involves placing a limited amount of product in selected retail outlets and monitoring its sales activity. If the concept still looks promising, a full-scale market test is initiated. This is the final phase, and it usually involves placing the new product in numerous retail outlets in an entire city. Analysis of test-market results dictates whether a new product goes into national distribution or on the scrap heap.

The first two phases, concept screening and concept testing, are much too complex and unpredictable to be appropriate small business selection tools. However, you can use a simplified version of pretest market testing (third phase) to your advantage. This should give you all the consumer market research information you'll need to make a sound decision. And the process is really quite easy.

You'll need a small quantity of your proposed product. Try to manufacture it at the lowest unit cost possible. If you can make a dozen or two dozen by hand in your basement, that's fine. But don't take a shortcut on quality. This limited production run must represent, as closely as possible, the true characteristics and appearance of your final product. If your product requires packaging, attempt a representative job in this area also. If necessary, have some labels printed up. You might even contact a few local packaging companies for assistance. They may be able to put together a couple dozen "samples" for you.

When your product is ready, visit a few retailers. You'll find that smaller, local business owners are usually more receptive to new ideas than the big chains. Explain that you have a new product that you'd like to test in their store. Offer them the product at about one-third of the retail selling price. This disproportionately high profit margin may be all that it takes to win them over. If not, offer them the product for free with the understanding that they will sell it at the price you specify. Guarantee that you'll stand behind any customer complaints or problems. Make it clear that your only interest is to find out how salable the product is at a given price. It is to be hoped that the business owner's interest and curiosity may also be aroused.

A short time after your product is on the shelf, you should begin to get results. Good or bad. Ask your retailer to compare the movement of your product with similar items that have been sold in the past. If your product is a winner, the retailer's enthusiasm will tell you so. But if the results are marginal or totally negative, consider yourself lucky. It's much better to know now than after you have invested a large amount of money in production facilities and business start-up expenses.

MARKET ANALYSIS AND CONCLUSIONS

When you reach this point in the analysis of a specific business opportunity, all your market information gathering will have been completed. You'll have facts and opinions from secondary sources, personal interviews with numerous types of sources, and telephone interviews with several types of sources. You may also have site-location information or consumer market research results. In other words, you've got a vast amount of information. What are you going to do with it all? Well, it really has only one major purpose: to assist you in meeting your original objective. Let's just say for example that your objective was to analyze the fast-food franchises that are available and to select the one that offers the best opportunity. After stating this objective, you laid out your work plan, set up a time schedule, wrote your list of master questions, and went on to complete all the information-gathering work. Now it's time to do your analysis and make a selection. It is hoped that the evidence will be so one-sided that your selection is obvious. Or maybe you'll be lucky and have two exciting opportunities to choose from.

If your conclusion or choice is not obvious, however, the best and simplest way to reach a conclusion is to sort out all the information you've gathered by means of your master list of questions. Summarize all the information that relates to a question. This summary should give you the answer. If not, possibly some call-backs like the ones you may have made to small business owners are in order. When you have a concisely stated answer to each question on your master question list, you should be able to look at your stated objective and reach a decision.

If your decision is positive, there are only two more steps before you're in business. These are covered in the following sections.

FINANCIAL ANALYSIS

You may recall that large companies initiate a financial and legal analysis of an acquisition candidate if the results of the market analysis are positive. You'll want to do the same thing if you're planning to purchase an ongoing independent business or an ongoing franchise. And if you're planning to start a business, a financial analysis of a "similar" business that is for sale might not be a bad idea. You might be able to learn a lot from an ongoing business financial record. Just tell the owner that you're not sure if you want to buy an ongoing business or start a business from scratch. If the person offers to show you the financial record on that basis, you'll not have an ethical conflict. Maybe the records will look so appealing that you'll decide to change your mind and buy that business after all.

As is true in a market analysis, the first step in a financial analysis is to gather together all available financial information. This information is usually available in the following places: (1) financial statements, (2) tax returns, (3) other internal records, and (4) the seller's bank.

A seller should make internal records available to any serious prospective buyer. If the seller cannot, or will not, provide this information, it is grounds for concern. Either inadequate records are being kept or information is being withheld. In each case, exercise caution. The primary financial statements of any company are the balance sheet and the income statement. A balance sheet summarizes the financial position of a business at a given time, usually the end of a fiscal year. The income statement reflects the revenue and expenses of a business during a specific period of time, usually for a three-month or twelve-month period. These financial statements may be audited or unaudited. Audited statements should include a statement of the accounting firm's opinion.

Tax returns are also valuable sources of financial information. The federal and state income-tax returns of the proprietor or of the corporation should be made available for examination. The seller may have also filed payroll-tax reports, sales-tax reports, excise-tax reports, or other tax reports. Gather up whatever is available in the tax-return area.

There are usually many internal financial records that back up and support the balance sheet and income statement. These may include sales records, accounts receivable, purchases, accounts payable, cash-flow statements, and operating budgets. If the company is in manufacturing, cost-control reports including material cost, labor cost, and overhead may also be available.

The seller's bank is the last major source of financial information. The bank can supply information on cash deposits and short- and long-term loans. You'll probably need the seller's approval to obtain access to this type of information.

All information (annual statements, etc.) should be requested for a ten-year period, and a minimum of three years is probably essential. If the company is less than ten years old, financial statements for the entire life of the company should be gathered.

All the financial information that you are able to collect is extremely valuable to make a sound analysis. But even good information can be misinterpreted or misunderstood. Analysis of financial information is probably best done by a professional accountant. If you're not qualified in this area, it's a good idea to seek professional assistance. Although you will probably want to maintain responsibility for gathering information from the seller, do put it in the hands of an accountant who is capable of a thorough and meaningful analysis. If you're interested in more detailed information in this area, a very useful treatment of small business financial analysis is included as part of a booklet published by the SBA and entitled *Buying and Selling a Small Business.*

LEGAL ANALYSIS

The single most important step you can take concerning the legal analysis of a potential business purchase is to get a *good lawyer.* Having a good lawyer is probably even more critical than having a good accountant. Most of us have, or can develop, some competency in keeping and analyzing financial records. This is not true for legal matters. And even if it were, it's illegal to practice law without a license.

The emphasis in the first sentence of this section on the word *good* cannot be overemphasized. What you want is a good lawyer, and good is not necessarily synonymous with expensive. Rather, good means knowledgeable, conscientious, thorough, and timely. Finding a good lawyer is important because a not-so-good-lawyer can really do you harm in the purchase of a small business. If the lawyer fails to do a good job, you may not even be buying all the essential assets of the business, or your management options may be severely limited when you take over its operation. Another reason you'll want to select a good lawyer, if you need any more reasons, is that you'll need a lawyer to perform certain functions as long as you own a business. And it's not wise, nor is it easy, to hopscotch between lawyers. A lawyer's exposure and experience with your particular situations and problems over a period of time become almost indispensable.

It's not easy to choose a good lawyer. If a friend (whom you trust) makes a solid recommendation, that's probably a safe bet. Otherwise, I'd solicit advice from maybe five or six small business owners. You can go back to some of the owners you met with in the past or you can approach some new ones. Simply explain that you're looking for a competent lawyer who appears to enjoy dealing with small business situations (many lawyers do not). Ask them who their lawyers are and ask for any other names that they've heard good things about. You can probably make all these contacts by phone.

Now choose the two or three that sounded best and meet with them. Ask about their small business experience. Try to get to know them personally. A client-lawyer relationship is very personal at times. You'll want a lawyer whom you can get along with easily, although, in most cases, it's not a good idea to associate socially with your lawyer.

You'll probably want to assume two roles in the legal analysis phase of a small business purchase. You'll probably be the primary interface between your lawyer and the seller. In this role you'll do much of the information gathering. Your lawyers will know the kind of information to look for. Some major areas include contracts with suppliers, customers, creditors, employees, lessors, and others. You'll also be interested in insurance policies, evidence of ownership, organization documents, and so on. Your lawyer will probably investigate external records such as the office of records, tax authorities, zoning ordinances, building codes, and court records.

The second role you will assume in the relationship with your lawyer is that of decision maker. It is the lawyer's purpose to present you with an intelligent analysis and statement of the alternatives. Ultimately, it is you who should make the decisions. After all, it's your name that goes on the dotted line labeled "buyer."

MAKING A DECISION

At this point in the analysis process, there is little left to do but make a decision. All the evidence (both good and bad) is in. The market analysis, financial analysis, and legal analysis have been completed for a specific business opportunity. The decision boils down to either investing in that franchise, starting that business, or buying that ongoing business.

There are several things you might keep in mind during your deliberation. First, try to remain as impartial and objective as possible. Remember, I mentioned earlier that most big businesses are very good at this. This is an area where it might be a good idea to try to emulate, as much as possible, one of the slight edges that being big has in the decision-making process.

Also, it's probably a good idea at this time to analyze a financial forecast or *pro forma* statement of the specific opportunity you're contemplating. You may have done this as part of your financial analysis, but if not, do it now. Remember, financial records such as balance sheets and income statements are just recorded history, whereas a financial forecast or *pro forma* statement (a forecast for a new business) gives you a look at the future. Of course it's an estimate, but estimates, especially for short periods of time, such as one year, are often very reliable. Quite frequently you can require the seller to prepare a financial forecast for you. If so, use it as input, not as the final estimate. Ask the seller to explain how it was developed and what assumptions it is based on, then make your own adjustment, if appropriate.

The final thing to keep in mind is the advice and counsel of your accountant, your lawyer, your spouse, and your trusted friends. Talk to them as much as necessary until you feel comfortable with your decision.

In the next three chapters you'll see how to apply the techniques presented in this chapter to specific franchise opportunities, start-up opportunities, and ongoing opportunities.

11

SELECTING A
FRANCHISE
OPPORTUNITY

If you have built castles in the air, your work need not be lost,
that is where they should be. Now put foundations under them.
HENRY DAVID THOREAU

If your business type selection is some form of franchise, then this
is the chapter for you. You'll see how to utilize the approach
described in the last chapter to make your specific franchise
selection.

Actually selecting a franchise opportunity is quite easy, and in
many instances it's too easy. This may sound absurd, but companies that use franchising (franchisors) as a method of distribution are actually promoting, and in a few instances "hustling,"
their franchises, just as car dealers are selling their cars and real
estate agents are selling their houses. Franchisors do their best,
and rightly so from their point of view, to make their franchise
opportunity look very attractive to potential franchisees.

And you, as a potential franchisee, should try to avoid being
"sold" too easily. You've got to penetrate the friendly handshakes
and congeniality. You've got to get down to the facts of the situation. Probably the best way to do this is to assume the position of
a cautious and careful buyer. Establish the attitude that you are
selecting them, rather than that they are selecting you. This
doesn't have to mean that you come across as aloof and arrogant.

Instead, you will appear more as a clean-thinking and careful business manager.

I don't want you to get the impression from the preceding comments, however, that franchisors are con artists. On the contrary, most franchising companies are fine organizations that offer a legitimate and well-conceived business opportunity.

Franchising is really a very old system of distribution. Automobile manufacturers and oil companies have been franchising their retail outlets since the early days of passenger cars. Even though most of us think of fast-food restaurants when we think of franchises, the traditional franchise (automobile dealership, gasoline station, and soft-drink bottler) still account for about half of all franchise outlets and about three-quarters of all franchise dollar sales.

However, it is the newer forms of franchises (for example, fast food, convenience stores, campgrounds, rental services, printing and copying services, etc.) that are leading in growth. The Department of Commerce publication *Franchising in the Economy, 1973–75* reports a 15 percent increase in number of outlets and a 26 percent increase in sales for newer types of franchising during this two-year period. In comparison, sales for traditional franchisors, during this same two-year period, increased by a modest 5 percent. Of course, these are industry totals. No solid conclusion concerning the growth of a specific franchise opportunity (traditional or newer type) should be drawn from these statistics.

IDENTIFYING SPECIFIC FRANCHISE
OPPORTUNITIES

You now know that you're interested in a specific type of franchise opportunity—fast food or auto repair or rental service or whatever. The first step in selecting a specific franchise opportunity is to identify all the different franchises that are available in your specific area of interest. It turns out that there are numerous places to look. A brief description of each follows.

Several franchise directories are available that list franchise offers in addition to specific details on each, such as cost, number of franchises, and so forth. The two most popular are *Directory of Franchising Organizations* published by Pilot Industries and *Franchise Opportunities Handbook* published by the U.S. Department of Commerce.

An excellent source of franchise opportunities is newspaper and magazine ads. In this category, the Sunday edition of your local newspaper may be most helpful. My personal favorite is the Thursday edition of the *Wall Street Journal*. This edition has a special portion of its classified section devoted to franchise-opportunity advertising.

Another source is small business opportunity and franchise shows. At these shows you'll find booths set up by franchisors to provide information and literature. These shows are held once or twice a year in major cities.

The yellow pages are another good source. Just look under the classified listing that you're interested in. You can then call a local franchisee and ask for the address of the headquarters office. Write them for information.

Many of the newer franchise companies rely on advertising to attract new franchisees and to make it convenient for you to respond to ads. Companies often will include a toll-free phone number or ask you to call their headquarters collect. Go ahead and call, but don't expect much on this first inquiry. At best, you'll probably get a secretary who will offer to send out a package of information. At worst, you'll get an answering service that will also offer to send you a package of information. In most cases, you will be informed that a representative will telephone you after you've had a chance to look over the mailed information. Obviously, for job security reasons, it's wisest to give them only your home phone number.

Don't assume that because a franchisor is not actively soliciting franchisees (through advertisements or shows) that it is not interested in additional prospects. Many franchise companies are just so well known, and have such a reputation for success, that they don't have to solicit. Potential franchisees approach them constantly. If you're interested in a big-name hamburger franchise, go ahead and send a brief letter noting your interest to

McDonald's and Burger King. You have nothing to loose and everything to gain.

THE FRANCHISOR'S FIRST CONTACT

The variety of contact methods used by franchising companies is surprising. Probably the most common is the friendly, yet businesslike, phone call. The primary purpose of this call is to let you know that the company is responsive and to do some preliminary screening of candidates. After some chitchat, the company representative will ask why you're interested in this company's franchise. Then you'll be asked to supply some background information on yourself, for instance, your age, family situation, present job, and other types of work experience you've had. Finally, the representative may want to know how much money you're able to invest. Be prepared to answer all these questions in a brief but thorough manner. At the close of the conversation, the company representative will ask to meet with you, or if the person feels the need for more information, will ask you to send in the questionnaire that was in the packet of information you received.

But many franchising companies take a different approach. They let you make the first contact. Based on the information they've sent you, you'll be asked to call for further information or to send in the enclosed questionnaire. This way they feel that you're at least somewhat interested before they expend any effort on you.

Then there's what I call the "hard-sell" approach. After your package of information arrives, you'll get a call from a very persistent company representative. I once got this kind of a call, told the caller I wasn't interested in the franchise, and at two-week intervals received follow-up calls from the same rep, to see if I'd changed my mind. Each time I was invited on an expense-paid trip to headquarters, if I sent in the questionnaire form and it was approved. Be prepared to encounter the "hard-sell" once in a while. And remember that the harder someone tries to sell something, the less it probably is worth.

Incorporated in the questionnaire used by most franchise companies is a net-worth section. It may be called financial data, or a financial statement, or even a personal net-worth statement. Whatever it's called, it should present no problem to you. You've already completed the same form in your self-analysis in Chapter 3. Just remember to fill in this section honestly and completely. If you don't have sufficient capital, the franchisor will find out eventually, so you might as well be truthful. Sometimes franchisors are in a position to offer low-interest loans to undercapitalized franchisee candidates.

YOUR FIRST MEETING

There's a good chance that if a franchisor decides to meet with you, you are a likely candidate to be offered a franchise. A preliminary positive assessment has been made of you, based on phone discussions and the information in your questionnaire. This is especially true if you're invited to take an out-of-state trip to company headquarters. They will be making their final decision on you at this meeting. And at the same time, you should be gathering information and making some initial judgments about them, because this visit is really the first step in your franchise analysis and selection process.

Plan to contact enough franchising companies so that you will end up with at least three, and preferably five, personal visits. This may sound excessive, but it's the only way to make informed comparisons. After all, if you were interviewing for a new job, you'd probably talk to at least three or four companies. The same should hold true in this situation.

Speaking of job interviewing, you're probably going to get that feeling, the feeling that you're being interviewed for a job, during your franchisor meeting. The feeling is probably accurate, because you're being evaluated to run a portion of what the franchisor considers to be "its network of stores." The franchisor's future income and success depends on how well you and other new franchisees do. The franchisor must be careful, and some will even require you to take a written examination, just as employers often do.

After all, one of the attractive features of a franchised business opportunity is the security and know-how offered by the strength and name-brand reputation of the franchising company. This know-how and brand reputation lowers the risk of failure for you. But in exchange for this lower risk, franchisees must be willing to sacrifice some freedom. In fact, many franchising companies don't want franchisees who demand a great deal of freedom and independence. This is illustrated by a comment made to me by an executive of a major franchising company. This franchising company representative said something like: "We're not looking for generals who want to do everything their own way, we're looking for sergeants. Sergeants can exercise good judgment, but they can also follow sensible directives."

You'll have two purposes to accomplish during each franchisor visit. The first, obviously, is to make a good impression. Be pleasant, polite, but above all be yourself, by acting natural. Your second purpose is to gather all the information and ask all the questions you can. If this is done properly and politely, it will not be resented. Rather, you will be recognized as thorough and conscientious.

In many cases, the following information will be offered to you, but if not, ask for it:

- Annual report (if company is publicly held)
- A copy of the franchise agreement
- A table explaining the distribution of the franchisee fee and the initial capital investment
- Income-statement forecast of a typical franchisee

The list of questions you'll want to ask is not as short. As is true in any interview situation, try to blend the questions into the flow of conversation. You'll probably be meeting with more than one person during your visit. This will give you the opportunity to divide up the questions, so it will appear as though you're not being overly inquisitive. Here's the list of questions to ask, roughly in the order of easier questions first:

- How long has the company been in business? When did it award its first franchise? How many franchises are there now? Are they distributed regionally or nationally?

- At what rate have franchisees been added in the past? How many new ones are planned for this year? Next year?

- What policy changes—specifically related to new products, advertising programs, and franchisee services—are being considered for the near future?

- How does the franchisor view the competition? Which is largest? Most aggressive? Is any new competition appearing on the horizon? What are competitors' strengths and weaknesses?

- If the franchising company is privately held, ask about the major shareholders. Were they the original founders?

- How much, and what kind of, assistance is supplied to new franchises to establish facilities? Are facilities usually purchased or leased? Is a feasibility study of the location provided? How about construction guidance and assistance?

- What territorial rights are associated with a franchisee? Is the franchisee exclusive or nonexclusive? In a two-step distribution system, are you being offered a distributorship or a dealership?

- If any portion of the initial franchise cost is financial, what is the interest rate? Is any of the initial cost refundable in case of cancellation?

- How many franchises have failed? Is the failure rate changing? What explanation does the franchisor give for these failures?

- Ask for names and addresses of operating franchises in markets similar to ones you are considering. Also ask for names and addresses of franchisees that have failed. (There should be no hesitance to supply these.)

- Has a franchise ever been assigned in the market you're considering? If so, what was its fate? If it is in operation, ask if it would be all right to visit the owner.

- What is the initial training program like? How long does it last? Where is it held? Who pays for it? What topics are covered in the program? Are there any training aids available so you can train your employees?

- Is there an ongoing training program for franchises? If so, is it of a scheduled or impromptu nature? What sort of things are covered?

- For nonstore type franchisees, how is the selling accomplished? Door to door? Company-supplied leads? Prospecting? Do competitors use the same approach?

- Ask for an explanation of the franchisor's advertising program. Is there an advertising and promotion package for local advertising by the franchisee? Is a local advertising agency required or suggested?

- What services and ongoing assistance are offered by the franchising company? Ask about central purchasing, problem analysis, field service personnel, order expediting, and so on.

It's quite a list, isn't it? But all the questions are important. I'd suggest that you copy them down on one sheet or several sheets of paper and then take the list along with you on each visit. If you don't have time to ask all the questions, don't be overly concerned. You'll probably be invited to telephone collect if you have any additional questions. So just wait a few days and call them up!

FRANCHISING-COMPANY ANALYSIS

After your initial meeting with a franchisor, you'll be ready to begin a detailed investigation and analysis of that franchise opportunity. Each step in process is described in this section. It follows the same basic approach presented in the last chapter, except that now the focus is specifically on franchise-opportunity analysis. Before beginning the analysis itself, it is a good idea to lay out a work plan and timetable as described in the last chapter. The topics in this section are presented in the same sequence that your work plan and timetable should follow. Don't set up a "crash" schedule. It is far better to proceed carefully and thoughtfully.

Master List of Questions. The first step in analyzing a specific franchise opportunity is to compose a master list of questions. Actually, you're off to a very good start, because all the questions you ask in your visits with the franchisors should go on your master list. The additional questions are directed at assessing the success, reputation, and image of the franchising company. Since these additional questions are so specifically directed, they are easy to formulate. For example:

- What is the reputation of the franchisor? Has it changed (better or worse) recently?

- How successful have the franchisees been? Would they "do it again" if given another chance?

- What do competitors think about the reputation and success of the franchisor being evaluated?

- How well does the franchisor rate with financial reporting services and such community agencies as the Better Business Bureau, chamber of commerce, and banks?

The questions all follow this same vein. It's probably best to move on to the next step, developing the specific sources of information, and then you'll see how easy it is to write an interview guide for each specific type of source.

Sources of Information.   The most striking aspect of the source of information, useful in evaluating a franchise opportunity, is that they are somewhat limited. For example, if you are evaluating a franchise opportunity with company A, useful sources of information may include:

- Secondary sources

- Company A franchisees

- Company A franchisee failures

- Competitive franchisors (e.g., company B and company C)

- Franchisees of companies B and C

- Local independent competition

- Customers of franchisees and independents

However, in some instances, such as a fast-food franchise, the last two sources on this list are almost meaningless. Local independent competitors in the fast-food field are rare, and if they do exist, they're typically small factors in the market. The customers of fast-food franchisees are not very helpful, since they wouldn't be customers if they didn't like the food and service. Thus, with a fast-food franchise, and with many other retailing type franchises, you end up with a fairly restricted list of sources. It boils down to secondary sources, franchisors, and franchisees. Fortunately, this is enough to make a sound decision.

Interview Guides.   The most important interview guide is the one to be used in your discussions with franchisees. You can use it for the franchisees of the company you're analyzing, for failed franchisees of the company you're analyzing, for competitive franchisees, and for local independent competition. The way you phrase the question, of course, won't be the same for each group of sources, but most of the topics will be the same. Here are the basic questions you should have on your franchisee guide. (Add any others you feel are necessary for your particular situation.)

- When did you buy this franchise? What was your background and prior experience?

- What were you looking for in this franchise?

- What is your territory—is it exclusive?

- What is your personal work schedule? Does it vary much from day to day? When are the most busy periods?

(These early questions are designed to develop some background information and also to "ease into" some of the more touchy questions.)

- Exactly what products and services does your franchisor supply to you? Is the delivery timely?

- Who do you consider your strongest competition? Why? What do they do better than your franchisor?

- How would you characterize your relationship with your franchisor? Has it changed of late? Is their product-quality good?

- How often do they visit you? Do you consider most visits helpful or intrusions on your business?

- Do you have any specific problems with the franchisor?

- Any major problems with the business itself?

- What is your opinion of the company's national advertising program? What about local advertising assistance?

- How good was the company's training program? Is the training updated to keep pace with changes in the operation?

- Is the company's site-selection system good? How would you characterize the demographics of your site? Are you happy with this location? Why?

- What do you think of your fellow franchisees? Are they happy with their situations?

- Are you familiar with any franchisee failure in this chain? Why do you think they failed?

- Are you happy that you bought this franchise? Would you do it again today? Why? Why not?

- Can a franchise in this type of market area reach the sales-goal estimates made by the franchisor? How about the profit figures?

- Could you give me a rough estimate of the annual sales of your franchisee? What does it net before taxes?

- Is your sales volume growing? How much of this is price increases? Are your profits growing?

For your discussions with competitive franchisors, you can use the same list of questions you used in the initial meeting with the franchise you're evaluating. It will be most appropriate, because you will be visiting them with the understanding that you are interested in possibly purchasing a franchise from them, which is probably true. Remember, it's best to visit at least three or four franchisors, so each is a potential business-opportunity visit in addition to a competitive interview.

Unlike the fast-food or retailing franchise, many franchise types do have customers that make valuable sources of information. Personnel agency franchises, for example, provide a service to companies that are hiring new employees. A personnel manager or an assistant at these client companies would be able to discuss the reputation and quality of service provided by various franchised personnel placement agencies. A short interview guide, with primarily reputation type questions, may be helpful in structuring the discussion.

An interview guide is probably not needed for your discussions with secondary sources. Basically all you want to know is what they know about each of the franchise opportunities you're evaluating. Do franchising companies have good reputations? Are the secondary sources aware of any complaints concerning the franchisors? These are the kind of questions you'll want to ask.

Gathering Secondary-Source Information. There are about five basic secondary sources to check the reputation, image, and financial condition of the franchising companies you're evaluating. You can check the reputations and images with the local and national Better Business Bureau, your chamber of commerce, and the International Franchise Association, located in Washington, D.C. In addition to the annual report of a franchisor, there are two more sources to check for financial stability and strength. The first is a financial reporting service such as Dun and Bradstreet. Call your local Dun and Bradstreet office or ask your banker to assist you in obtaining reports on the specific companies. But don't rely completely on these reports. If the franchisors you're evaluating are publicly held, write to the Securities and Exchange Commission and request a copy of each company's 10-K report. This report, which goes into much more detail than the annual report, is especially useful if the annual report and/or the Dun and Bradstreet report show mixed results.

Don't make the mistake of assuming that simply because a franchising company is large it is financially sound. Just this year, one of the leading fried-chicken franchisors in the Chicago market declared bankruptcy. Don't take the chance of being the person who just opened his franchise the month before "the roof fell in."

Doing the Fieldwork. At this point in the analysis you will have completed about three to four initial visits with franchisors. Also, your secondary-source information gathering will be in progress or completed. This fieldwork phase is the most time-consuming and probably the most important aspect of franchise business-opportunity analysis. The sources you will be contacting include:

- Franchisees (of the three or four companies you visited)

- Failed franchises (of the three or four companies you visited)

- Independent competitors to franchisees

- Customers of franchisees (if appropriate)

The obvious question arises concerning the appropriate number of contacts to make in each category. It would be nice if there were some hard and fast rule, but there is none. It depends on how many contacts it takes to get consistent responses and complete answers to all your important questions. That is, it depends on your becoming comfortable with the information. It may take you only two or three visits with franchisees of a specific company to "be sure" that the franchisor was stretching the truth a little too far. Or maybe, after three or four visits with a company's franchisees, you will have consistent, glowing results. It's impossible to estimate the proper number of contacts beforehand, but in most situations it shouldn't take more than six contacts with a specific type of franchisor to reach a high level of confidence in the findings. But always be sure to do what your situation dictates. Too many contacts just cost more time, but too few could cost your life savings if they lead to a poor selection.

In the last chapter, the advantages and disadvantages of both personal interviews and telephone interviews were discussed. Although telephone interviews have their place, it's my personal opinion that the best way to make contacts in evaluating franchise opportunities is on a personal basis. I say this for two reasons. Number one, you'll be asking some very probing questions, questions that most people will hesitate to discuss on the telephone. And number two, franchisees are very busy people for the most part. It would be difficult to keep them on the phone long enough to complete your series of questions. For most franchise systems, you shouldn't have difficulty finding enough franchisees within driving distance of your home.

As is true of all personal interviews, you should call beforehand and make an appointment. It may be a good idea to use several approaches to explain the purpose of your visit. Often the direct approach is easiest—say something like: "I'm considering investing in one of your company's franchises. I spoke with Ms. Blank at headquarters last week, and she suggested that I visit several franchisees. Could I see you sometime this week?" The major shortcoming of this approach is that the franchisee will be biased to some extent by being a franchisee of the same chain you're considering. This might lead the person to avoid discussing with you the shortcomings of the franchise, or it might result in a "sour-grapes" session. A neutral approach might overcome some of the franchisee's prejudices. This would involve an explanation like, "I'm looking into several different franchise opportunities. I wonder if I could chat with you sometime this week?" If the person asks if you've been in touch with headquarters, just say, "Well, I've contacted several different franchising companies." The franchisee probably won't press it any further. The third, and final approach is to suggest that you're evaluating one of the franchisee's competitors. It goes something like: "I'm considering the purchase of a Blank franchise. I know that they're one of your competitors and I'd very much like to visit with you to understand your opinion of their operation. May I see you sometime this week?" This is not a total deception, because you probably are considering the purchase of a Blank franchise as well as the interviewee's franchise. But it will give you a different perspective during the discussion. After the person has discussed the competition, you can casually mention that you were also possibly considering buying a franchisee in this person's chain. All three approaches have their place. Use the ones that suit your situation and the type of perspective you need at the time.

If customer interviews are appropriate to your evaluation, it's probably best to arrange them by saying, "I'm looking into several franchise opportunities and I'd like to understand how you feel about several of them. May I stop in sometime this week for a brief visit?" With this approach you'll be assured of getting unbiased responses to your question, that is, if you're careful to ask the same questions about three or four competing companies.

In many cases, a franchisee's place of business is a very hectic and noisy operation. It's difficult, if not impossible, to carry out a good interview in this type of setting. I once tried to interview the owner of a hardware-store franchise in his store. It was a disaster. We were constantly being interrupted by customers asking for nuts and bolts or extension cords or advice on fixing leaking faucets. I offered to buy him lunch, but he was manning the store alone so he couldn't leave. After about an hour of interruptions I left instead, with very little accomplished. This problem can be avoided with careful planning. Seek out a place for your franchise discussions that is private and free of interruption. Suggest that it might be best to meet somewhere, like a restaurant for lunch or a coffee shop, or invite the person to your home for dinner. You might even be invited to the office the franchisee keeps at home. Arrangements concerning the meeting place can be handled when you call for the appointment. If all else fails and you must meet a franchisee at his or her place of business, and it's a busy place like a fast-food restaurant, be sure to make a firm appointment, for a slow time of day. Don't settle for a "drop in anytime" invitation. No doubt, if you do, your visit will come at a bad time. And if the owner doesn't have a private little hideaway, talk the person into chatting in your car. Then, at least, you will be free of most interruptions and the owner won't have to be concerned about employees overhearing everything that is said.

In addition to discussions with franchisees, visits to selected franchise locations are also essential. A brief visit to the location and a look around the neighborhood should be made before you meet with each franchisee. This way you'll be able to relate personally to their operation and also ask specific questions about their site selection. During your meeting, ask permission to "observe" each franchisee's operation sometime. Then visit these franchises later and watch what goes on. Plan to spend several hours at each one. Watch what the owner does, notice the types and number of customers, and drive around the area to get an idea of the income level and type of people in the immediate neighborhood.

Completing Your Analysis.   Depending on your specific situation, there are a few loose ends that may still need attention. The first is site-selection analysis. If you're buying a new store type franchise, this matter should not be your concern. One of the major strengths offered by franchisors is their experience and expertise in selecting franchise locations. If a franchisor does not provide site-selection analysis, be very cautious.

However, site selection could be of interest to you if you're considering the purchase of an ongoing franchise. If the franchise is very successful, then probably there is little reason to be concerned with its location. However, if you note some reason for concern, request a copy of the original analysis. Ask that it be updated if you're worried that a future zoning regulation or a planned expressway may divert much of the traffic from the location.

You should look into two other things if you're considering the purchase of an ongoing franchise: the financial and legal aspects of the purchase. Begin by rereading the pages in the last chapter that cover financial analysis and legal analysis, and then go about following the approach that is presented there. From a financial and legal viewpoint, buying an ongoing franchise is not that different from the purchase of any other type of ongoing business.

MAKING A SELECTION

The best and most straightforward way to make a franchise selection decision is first to take all the information you've gathered on a particular franchising company and look it over to see if it is complete and consistent. For example, remember the questions that were designed to determine the extent and reasons for franchisee failures. Simply stated these questions are:

1. How many franchises have failed in this chain?

2. Why have franchises failed?

These are both very important questions. Test the completeness of your analysis by making sure you have answers to these questions from as many sources as possible (the franchisor, franchisees, failed franchisees) and test the consistency of your analysis by checking to see if the answers from each source are basically the same. When you are confident about the completeness and consistency of your analysis, you can move on to the decision itself.

Presented below is a concise checklist that makes it possible to examine all the information gathered on a particular franchise offer. You should have answers to all the questions on the list for each specific franchise you've evaluated.

Checklist for Evaluating a Franchise Opportunity

1. Does the franchise appear to satisfy most of the elements of my business selection criteria?

2. Do I have the necessary capabilities to succeed in a franchise of this type?

3. Specifically, does the size and profitability of a typical franchise fulfill my income requirements?

4. Does the franchising company have a reputation for honesty and fair dealings?

5. Is the franchisor well established and experienced?

6. Is the franchising company successful and profitable?

7. Does it appear to have the management depth to continue operations indefinitely?

8. Have I been offered an exclusive franchise? If not, what guarantees do I have concerning sales potential?

9. Under what circumstances can I terminate the franchise contract? What costs are involved?

10. To whom and under what terms and conditions can I sell my franchise?

11. Is there a realistic and enduring need for this business in my area?

12. Can I meet local competition?

13. Is there a good chance of success in the territory offered me?

14. Has the franchisor investigated me thoroughly enough to guarantee itself that I can profitably operate one of its franchises?

15. Has there been a good percentage of success among new franchisees?

16. Does the franchisor have a good training program for me? For my employees?

17. Is the advertising, promotion, and merchandising program satisfactory?

18. Has a financial and legal analysis been completed with positive results?

After following the approach presented in this chapter, you should be able to answer all these questions for each of the franchise opportunities you've investigated, and the answers should make your selection fairly obvious.

There is the possibility that none of the franchise opportunities you analyze will meet your expectations. If so, my advice is to consider additional franchising companies, either in the same type of franchising (for example, fast food) or in some related area. For example, a related area to fast food would be franchised sit-down restaurants or 24-hour coffee shops. There are many fine franchising opportunities available, and they offer the chance for business success and personal fulfillment. If some additional effort is required to find that one opportunity that's right for you, the rewards in the long run will be worth the extra hours spent.

12

SELECTING AN ONGOING BUSINESS

When dealing with people, remember you are not dealing with creatures of logic, but with creatures of emotion, creatures bristling with prejudice and motivated by pride and vanity.

DALE CARNEGIE

There are a great many differences between a franchise and an independently owned, ongoing business. Let's take a look at some of the major differences, and then as we move farther into this chapter, you'll see how these differences affect the process of selecting an ongoing business.

The most striking difference between franchises and ongoing businesses is the one-of-a-kind nature of independent small businesses. All the franchises in a given chain are much the same. You know what to expect when you eat at a McDonald's or stay at a Holiday Inn. And to some extent, you know what to expect if you buy a McDonald's or a Holiday Inn franchise. Yet no two independent small businesses are even remotely alike. Two Italian restaurants, one called a Touch of Italy and the other called The Italian Village, may initially appear to offer the same business opportunity. A careful analysis of these two "similar" restaurants would probably reveal that a variation of the word *Italy* in the name is the only thing they have in common.

Unlike a franchise, an independent business does not have the "umbrella" of know-how and guidance offered by a franchisor. Because of this, the selection of an ongoing business must be made on the basis of what you, and you alone, can make of it in the future. What you can do with it in the years to come overshadows what the seller has done with it in the past.

Another major difference between selecting a franchise and selecting an ongoing independent business is the purchase price. Each franchisor has a fixed purchase price for its franchises. There are no negotiations and there are no questions of valuation. Independent businesses are quite the opposite. The seller is trying to get all he or she can, and the buyer should be trying to pay as little as possible. The fair market price for these two Italian restaurants mentioned earlier, even with the same seating capacity, could be thousands of dollars apart.

Site location is another factor that complicates many ongoing business selections. If the site is critical to the nature of the business, as in retailing, it should be analyzed before purchase. For all anyone knows, the site could have been selected originally because a friend of a friend in the real estate business knew of a storefront that was available. The store may be doing well now, but unexpected future changes in the neighborhood could result in a deteriorating situation.

The last major difference between selecting a franchise and an independent small business is time. There is much more pressure for a decision in the latter situation. Part of this time pressure stems from a sincere need to know on the part of the seller, but in many instances, time pressure is created artificially, either by an overly anxious buyer ("I've got to decide before someone else grabs it up") or by a high-pressure seller ("I've got to have an answer by next Wednesday. That's when my lease expires.").

Taken together, the differences that have just been discussed combine to make the selection of an ongoing independent business more challenging than the selection of a franchise. But to many, the rewards of total independence are worth it.

FINDING SPECIFIC PURCHASE OPPORTUNITIES

The first step in selecting a specific ongoing business opportunity is to identify specific purchase opportunities in the business type you previously selected.

There are several very effective ways to go about this. The most accessible source is newspaper classified advertisements. Most local newspapers have classified sections with a title something like "Business Opportunities for Sale." Large city newspapers have hundreds of individual ads in each Sunday edition. There are also numerous ads each day in the business-opportunity section of the *Wall Street Journal* classified pages. Usually, the businesses advertised for sale in the *Journal* are larger than the typical businesses found in local newspaper advertising.

Some real estate agencies handle small businesses. Those that do can probably best be located by scanning yellow-pages advertisements or by telephoning a few agencies at random. Most agencies are familiar with the type of listing handled by fellow brokers. In larger metropolitan areas, there are brokerage houses that specialize in selling small businesses. These agencies are typically referred to as business brokers. A quick look under this heading in your yellow pages will tell you if you have any business brokers in your area. Big-city business brokers tend to specialize in specific types of businesses. Some handle mostly manufacturing and job shop operations. Others are mainly involved in restaurants or retailing businesses. So if you have several to choose from, a phone call to each to determine their speciality may be necessary. There's another reason to contact more than one broker. In many areas, all business listings are exclusive to the agency that has that listing. So in order to be exposed to all the opportunities that are available, each of the agencies should be contacted. If you're interested in rural or out-of-state business opportunities, a national cooperative listing agency such as United Farm Agency may be helpful.

Another very good source of ongoing business opportunities is trade journals and newspapers. You're already familiar with the publications in your selected business area. A periodic review of classified advertisements in these publications may uncover some good leads.

Many potential sellers of businesses rely solely on word-of-mouth advertising to make it known. There are many legitimate reasons for this tactic. At times an employer doesn't want employees to know about the potential sale or might feel that knowledge of the owner's intention to sell might jeopardize relations with suppliers or customers. So if you have contacts in your particular field of interest, let it be known that you're interested in buying this or that kind of business. You never know, some evening you might get a telephone call from a potential seller. Lawyers and accountants are often used as conduits in "for-sale" word-of-mouth advertising. Touching base with any contacts you have in these fields may be fruitful.

There's one last way to find opportunities. It's a real long shot, but if it works, you'll have an inside track on a particular situation. Say, for example, you're looking for a men's clothing store, and there's one you've always admired in your town. There's no harm in calling up the owner, introducing yourself, and saying, "I'm interested in buying a clothing store. Have you, by any chance, ever considered selling?"

Through any and all of these sources, you should be able to identify a number of business opportunities in your selected business type. The next step is to narrow down the prospects by separating the good ones from the not-so-good ones.

MAKING CONTACT

Your initial visit with a business owner who wants to sell is very important. It's probably a good idea to get some preliminary information about each prospect on the phone. If direct contact with the owner is not possible, the broker probably will suffice. Specifics about the type of operation, annual sales, and the location of the business are probably enough to decide if a visit is worthwhile.

The purpose of your initial visit with a seller is to learn enough so that after this visit you will be able to make your first critical decision. That decision is whether to initiate an evaluation of the business or to scratch it off your list. Sometimes the place will look so bad that you'll know before you get out of the car that you don't want anything to do with it. At other times the decision may be quite agonizing.

Obviously, you'll need some information on which to base a judgment. Observation of the operation and a casual discussion with the owner will allow you to learn a lot. Is the equipment up to date and in good repair? Are things clean and tidy? Is the activity level indicative of a healthy, profitable business? Does the company's product or service seem in line with industry practice? Does the owner seem proud of the operation? And don't forget to make an assessment of the owner's business capabilities and integrity.

In addition to observation and casual discussion, some specific questions are in order. Ask about the history of the business—when it was started and by whom, how it grew and developed. Ask the pointed question "Why are you selling?" You'll probably get a rehearsed answer that may or may not be true, but note it anyway. There will be more later in the chapter on the necessity for knowing the real reason a business is for sale. Of course, you'll want to determine the asking price and specifically what assets are involved in the sale. The building itself is the most obvious asset that may or may not be included. Less obvious items include patents, licenses, subsidiary companies, and so forth. Then, last but not least, confirm the gross annual sales figure, and ask for last year's and this year's estimated, net pretax income. Be sure to clarify whether the owner's salary is counted in the income figure. If not, ask for it separately.

Earlier I mentioned that some businesses will turn you off the instant you see them, but the opposite can happen too. It's called "love at first sight." Try your best to avoid this potentially disastrous infatuation. Another pitfall is being pressured into a premature decision. A true story in the next section illustrates how a hasty decision can often go sour.

THE RESULTS OF A HASTY DECISION

Jim Schwartz took a job as a sales engineer with a large oil company in Chicago after he graduated from college. Several years later, he resigned to go back to school for a master's degree in business. His wife provided the necessary financial support. In the last semester of his academic program, Jim decided that he would like to try a business of his own, after graduation. But to keep his option open, he did participate in the campus recruiting program. As graduation approached, Jim was sure he'd be able to find a business where he could apply his capabilities, so he turned down three attractive job offers.

In June, Jim began his search for the right company. One of Jim's professors put him in touch with several lawyers and business brokers who were active in the small business community. He also checked newspaper ads each day for possible opportunities. By the end of June, Jim had uncovered, explored, and rejected about seven or eight prospects. These included a restaurant—Jim didn't like the heavy weekend work schedule; a new business venture to make portable kitchen appliances—too many major competitors; a fishing-tackle manufacturer—family-owned business that wanted a manager but did not wish to sell any portion of the equity; and a small bottling company—overcapacity in the market area. By examining the financial records of several of these companies, Jim realized that in many cases they were incomplete and potentially misleading.

At a get-together on the Fourth of July weekend, a friend of Jim's father told Jim of another opportunity. It was Custom Industries, a small packaging converter that specialized in printing and forming small paper boxes for consumer products. The founder and owner, Bill Kusper, was in need of additional financing and was willing to sell a portion of his equity to get it.

Early that next week, Jim visited with Bill Kusper. Bill seemed like a very capable and experienced sales type. But based on what Jim saw and heard, Kusper had seriously neglected the production side of the business. There were some areas that obviously could be improved—changes that would help plant efficiency, for example. Kusper let it be known to Jim that because of the urgent need for cash, there was not much time available for analysis and procrastination. In fact, he gave Jim ten days to make a decision. Jim made a brief market check and quickly determined that Custom Industries products served many growing consumer product areas such as cosmetics, toiletries, and so on. Jim then checked over the books and discovered some problems. He found some poor credit risks among the accounts receivable. He also found two different versions of the latest quarterly income statement. A check of the inventory revealed $4000 or more of virtually obsolete items.

It's hard to believe, but based on this mixed information, Jim made an offer to Kusper one week after his initial visit. He felt the company could be made into a profitable business with his operating skills and the infusion of his new capital. In exchange for $20,000, Jim bought a quarter equity interest in Custom Industries. Jim took over the day-to-day plant operations, and Bill Kusper was to devote his full time to sales.

It wasn't long before things began to go wrong. First a $3000 bill to a major supplier surfaced. It hadn't been recorded. Next, Jim discovered that first-quarter federal withholding and Social Security taxes had been withheld from employee paychecks but had not been paid to the government. This resulted in another $1500 liability. In addition to all the operational responsibilities, Jim discovered that he was also handling all the in-house sales coordination activities. And he soon discovered why Bill Kusper didn't really have much time available for selling the products of Custom Industries. Kusper, it turned out, was also the owner of a used-car lot, and that's where he spent most of his time. In fact, he was so busy buying and selling cars that he was totally ignoring his sales responsibility at Custom Industries.

Maybe Jim should have followed that old saying "Never trust a used-car salesman." But how was Jim to know. He didn't even investigate the situation thoroughly enough to find out that Kusper was a used-car salesman! Jim confided afterward that his major mistake was his hasty approach. "If I were to do it over again," he said, "I'd talk to everyone so I'd be sure of knowing the complete story."

PLANNING YOUR ANALYSIS

If your initial contact with a business owner results in a decision to initiate an evaluation, the next step is to plan the analysis. But before getting involved in this step, there is a key point that should be kept in mind. It's important to recognize that it will probably be necessary to initiate an analysis of several, or even a half a dozen, businesses before you find the one that suits you. As a result, you should build informal review and decision points into the analysis of a particular business. The purpose of these decision points is to give you a chance to step back and ask the question "Based on what I know now, does this still look like a promising opportunity?" If at any point your answer is no, then you'll have the flexibility to terminate the analysis. If your answer is yes, then you can proceed to the next part of the analysis. It's not necessary to actually plan exactly when these "go" or "no-go" decisions will be made. In fact it's probably best to always keep in mind the possibility of cutting off analysis at any time. With this approach you'll be sure your time and energy are always being expended on efforts that could result in a purchase.

As with the analysis of any business opportunity, it's essential to define each of the major steps required and to tie a time schedule to the completion of these steps. The major step necessary for a comprehensive analysis of an ongoing, independent business are:

1. Gathering of sales, financial, tax, and any other records that are available from the subject company

2. Market analysis:

   - Develop a list of all questions that need answering.

   - Develop a list of Sources of Information.

   - Write Interview Guides.

   - Gather Market Information (Fieldwork).

   - Site analysis and consumer product testing (if applicable).

   - Analyze data and reach market conclusions.

3. Financial analysis

4. Legal analysis

Depending on time limitations, it may be desirable to initiate the financial and legal analysis while the market analysis is in progress. This could be most appropriate if early market analysis findings are extremely positive.

Obviously, a preliminary review of the main financial document should be made before any time or effort is committed to the market analysis. The main purpose of this review is to become familiar with the numbers, to confirm company size and profitability figures. However, financial information for many small businesses does not accurately portray either the current position or future potential of the business. In fact, some business brokers initially hesitate to show prospective buyers copies of financial statements because "the statements would turn off too many potential buyers. Nobody would buy on the basis of some of these statements." In many situations you're really buying potential rather than current earnings. So don't be totally turned off if the statements are less than attractive.

MARKET ANALYSIS

The specific steps of the market analysis were listed above. This listing is in the sequence that it should be performed. Specific details relating to each step were the main focal point of the material presented in Chapter 10. It may be helpful to refer back to pages 116 thru 131 in Chapter 10 to refresh your memory.

The essence of a successful market analysis of an ongoing, independent business is to identify the right people to talk to and then to ask them the right questions. First, let's spend some time on the issue of identifying the right people. There is no way I can specifically point out to you who are the right people to talk to for your specific analysis. There are just too many different kinds of businesses and kinds of situations. But I can give you a very helpful guideline for identifying the right people.

Who the right people are depends mostly on the level of distribution that the business occupies. There are four levels in a traditional distribution system, as shown in Figure 12. Each is represented by a box.

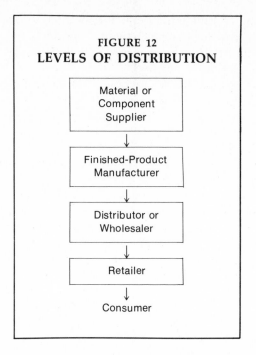

FIGURE 12
LEVELS OF DISTRIBUTION

Material or
Component
Supplier

↓

Finished-Product
Manufacturer

↓

Distributor or
Wholesaler

↓

Retailer

↓

Consumer

Almost all businesses function at one of these levels. For example, appliance stores and hardware stores are obviously retailers, and retailers, like appliance stores and hardware stores, usually purchase products and service parts from distributors and wholesalers. Wholesalers and distributors usually get their products from finished-product manufacturers. And finished-product manufacturers purchase materials and components from their supplier. You may be wondering how service companies, those that sell no products, like dry cleaners, fit in. Service businesses usually function at the retail level, in that customers of service companies are the consumer or end user of the service. Restaurants also function at the retail level.

What has all this got to do with finding the right people to talk to? A lot, because the right people to talk to are all those individuals or businesses that are above, alongside, or below your target business in the distribution system. Let's take an appliance distributor, for example. Say this distributor, called Ace Appliance Distributing, is the company you're considering purchasing. The right people to talk to are retailers, both customers and noncustomers of Ace (these are below Ace); appliance manufacturers, both of lines distributed by Ace and competitors' lines (these are above Ace); and other appliance distributors, Ace's competitors (these are beside Ace).

By using the above, below, and beside guideline, it's fairly easy to define the right people to talk to:

For Retailers:

• Consumers

• Fellow retailers

• Distributors/wholesalers

For Distributors/wholesalers:

• Retailers

• Fellow distributors/wholesalers

• Finished-product manufacturers

For Finished-Product Manufacturers:

• Distributors/wholesalers

• Manufacturers representatives (possibly)

• Fellow manufacturers

• Material or component suppliers

For Material or Component Suppliers:

- Finished-product manufacturers

- Fellow suppliers

- Vendors to the material or component suppliers

In each of these cases, the "fellow business owners" or competitors are the most important and critical sources of information. They know as much or more about the business as the potential seller and are probably less biased, since they are not trying to "sell" their company.

In the above discussion I've been using the expression right *people* to talk to, when I've really been identifying the right companies to talk to. But identifying the right people, once you've found the right companies, is really quite simple. For companies "above" in the distribution system, sales people are best because they are the ones who directly see the seller's company as a customer. For companies "beside" in the distribution system, you probably want the owner or another principal officer, preferably in marketing or sales. And finally, for companies "below," the person responsible for the purchasing function is the right person.

In addition to the *right* people to talk to (the most important contacts), there is also a secondary group of contacts that can be quite useful. This group, which is much the same for all market analysis situations, is highlighted below:

- Key employees of the seller's company: if the company you're analyzing is large enough, key employees (besides the owner) may be useful. Examples include the sales manager and production manager.

- Ex-employees: if you're lucky enough to find a talkative ex-employee, don't pass up the chance to "buy the person a cup of coffee."

- The banker or other institution who has been involved in loans to the seller's company

- Chamber of commerce

- Better Business Bureau

- Dun and Bradstreet

- Securities and Exchange Commission—if the company is publicly held

Now that the right people to talk to have been identified, the right questions to ask them become the important consideration. Basically, you want to know everything that they know about the market and the seller's company that is relevant to the purchase decision. You don't need to know any more, and you dare not find out anything less. Let's look at each level in the distribution system and see what it knows that's relevant to the purchase decision.

First, the level below, which are the seller's customers, ex-customers, and potential customers. This group knows such relevant things as:

- The quality of the products or services offered by the seller

- The prices charged by the seller and competitors

- How much product they're buying and from whom

- The reputation and reliability of the seller and competitors

- If their requirements for the products or services are going to increase or decrease in the future

- The personal reputation and integrity of the seller

- Why they buy from whom they buy (be it price, quality, service, friendship, etc.)

The level above the seller's company, or the seller's suppliers, ex-suppliers, and potential suppliers, know such things as:

- If the seller is in a position to take advantage of trade discounts
- How promptly the seller pays bills
- How much and what the seller "buys" compared to competition
- If the seller is fair and equitable in dealings
- If the quantity purchased by the seller has changed and why
- The prices paid by the seller and competition
- If the seller is keeping up with changes in the market and technology
- The growth or shrinkage of the market for the seller's products

And the people beside the seller, the competitors, know the most important thing:

- If the market as a whole is growing and how much
- If profits are shrinking or expanding
- The overall likely size of the market
- If the seller's share is shrinking or expanding and why
- The percentage of sales that go to rent, cost of goods sold, advertising, sales representatives' commissions, and so forth
- The reputation of the seller
- The seasonality of the business

- Whether the competitor would "buy in" to this business or "do it all over again" if the chance arose

- The strengths and weaknesses of each major competitor, including the seller

All these relevant "knowns" translate directly into questions during the visits with the right people. Ask them all, and more if necessary. One other question to answer is the key question you've already asked the seller. Why is the business for sale? You may not be able to ask this question directly to all the people you're interviewing (some may not know the business is for sale), but always keep this question in mind. Comments may be made in any discussion that will either confirm the seller's answer or lead you to the *real* reason.

Another important aspect of the market analysis of any ongoing business is an evaluation of the company's own internal sales records and preparation of a sales forecast. Input for the sales forecast will come from historic company trends and from information gathered in discussions with customers, competitors, and suppliers. The evaluation of the seller's internal sales records should include:

- Changes in gross margin from year to year

- An analysis of advertising expenditures

- An analysis of selling costs as a percentage of gross sales

- The company's year-to-year change in sales dollars

- An analysis of year-to-year price increases

- Seasonality and month-to-month sales changes

- Impact of business cycles on company sales

- Trends in average sales per customer

- Distribution of sales by key customers

A review of the internal records will also provide names and addresses of the seller's customers and suppliers. These, of course, will be very helpful in identifying contacts to be used in the fieldwork.

At the point where you're fairly sure the market analysis results will be positive, it's time to call in your accountant and lawyer. Then they can start on the financial analysis and legal analysis, in earnest. Don't call them in too early, or you may just end up paying for time on their "meter" that was spent on a company that you'll eventually decide not to buy because of poor market analysis results.

HOW MUCH TO PAY FOR A BUSINESS

As was mentioned at the beginning of this chapter, you as the buyer will want to pay as little as possible for the business of your choice. You already know the asking price. What you're not sure of is the fair market price and, specifically, at what price you can make a deal.

Some particular types of businesses have established formulas for determining a fair selling price. It would be well to inquire of business brokers and business owners if such a method exists in the type of business you're investigating. There are also some books that may be available at your local library that specifically deal with established methods of valuing particular types of businesses and properties. One of these is entitled *Guide to Buying or Selling a Business* (James M. Hanson, Prentice-Hall, 1975).

Beyond specific formulas and established tradition, there are two basic approaches for estimating a fair purchase price. The first method is generally referred to as capitalization of future earnings. You may be familiar with this approach from reading the financial press, because it is the method used in acquisitions by most big businesses. A modification of it is also used in the stock market. In this context, expressions such as "it's selling for five times current earnings" or "seventeen times estimated earnings" are common.

The capitalization of future earnings approach is based on two estimates. The first is an estimate of future annual earnings of the business, usually for five years into the future. The second estimate is a quantification of the risk associated with the business. This risk factor is usually estimated by comparing the business with the known risks of other types of investments. If the business is very stable and secure, for example, the risk might be similar to a bank savings account or U.S. Government bonds. Say this return is 5 percent. Then if the business has a five-year estimated future pre-tax profit of $5000 a year (after deducting the owner's salary), this approach would suggest a fair market price of $5000 divided by 0.05, or $100,000. However, if the risk is much higher, the risk factor might be estimated at 25 percent. Then the business would be valued at $5000 ÷ 0.25, or $20,000. Big business usually think in terms of return on investment rather than risk factor, but it's really the same process. In the last example, were this business to be purchased for $20,000 and were it to earn $5000 per year, the annual return on investment would be $5000 ÷ $20,000, or 25 percent. Either way, with risk factor or return on investment, the results are the same.

The second method of estimating a fair market price of an ongoing business is based on asset appraisal. The tangible assets most commonly involved in the transfer of a small business are inventory, office supplies, fixtures and equipment, and possibly real estate. The one intangible asset is goodwill. Valuation of all of the tangible assets is fairly straightforward, although an expert appraiser often is called in to assist on inventory, equipment, or real estate. After all these tangible assets are appraised, an additional value is added for goodwill. The term *goodwill* is a catchall for *all* intangible assets of the business. It includes such things as favorable location, customer lists, special connections with suppliers, good name, capable staff and personnel, good reputation for product quality and service, and so on. All these goodwill "assets" relate to the future earning power of the business. Typically, the value that is put on goodwill is less than half, and frequently only 10 or 20 percent of the total value of physical assets.

It may be obvious by now that both these methods have shortcomings. The capitalization of future earnings requires that both future earnings and a risk factor be estimated. This makes its application, in many situations, nothing more than a guessing game. The use of historical data to forecast earnings is often impossible because of the absence of good records or the absence of earnings, or the absence of both. Moreover, a relatively small change in the risk factor can significantly effect the resulting fair market price. A change from a 7 percent risk factor to a 14 percent risk factor, for example, cuts the price in half.

Because of the nebulous nature of this first method, the asset appraisal method is used most frequently. Of course, its major shortcoming is assignment of a mutually agreed value to goodwill. Potential buyers rightly value goodwill with respect to future earning potential. But sellers often want to associate the value of goodwill to past investments of time, effort, and money.

Happily, there is an approach which resolves some of the shortcomings of dealing with either method. It accomplishes this because it's actually a combination of the two. Anyway, it does seem to be the most reasonable, and I would advise its use in most instances. This combination approach, often called the "excess earning" method, starts by sharply differentiating the salary income of a business from the investment income of a business. That is, it assumes that buyers quite naturally look for a business that can earn a fair return on investment, after deducting a reasonable salary for themselves and for any time put in by their family. This "after-salary" income (or income potential) must be at least equal to the earning power of outside investments, or the buyer would have no interest in making a purchase.

Let's take a look at an example that shows how the excess profits method works. Assume that the tangible assets of a business are fairly valued at $100,000. We also know that the buyer is looking for a 10 percent return on investment, roughly comparable to the return expected from a high-quality common stock. Ten percent of the $100,000 asset value is $10,000 annual return, or profit on investment. The potential buyer feels that the full-time effort in running the business is worthy of a salary of $20,000 per year. Therefore, the buyer expects a pre-tax total net profit of $30,000 each year ($10,000 + $20,000). The next step is to compare this $30,000 figure with the actual (or anticipated) profit of the business. Say this well-established business, on the average, earns $32,000 a year. Subtraction results in an excess profit of $2000 ($32,000 − $30,000). By projecting this excess profit over some time period, the value of goodwill can be determined. The period-of-time multiplier depends on how long it would take to establish a similar business and bring it to a similar profitability level. Say the buyer places the value at three years. Then goodwill, in this example, has a value of $6000 (3 × $2000). So the fair market value of the business is $106,000 ($100,000 physical assets + $6000 goodwill).

Let's look at the implications of a lower average earnings figure. Assume, for example, that the business averaged a profit of only $25,000 instead of $32,000. Then the excess profits would be negative ($25,000 less $10,000 return on investment and $20,000 salary = −$7000). This negative excessive profits says one of several things:

1. The assets have been valued too high, or

2. The assets are incapable of earning a 10 percent return, or

3. The business is not capable of supporting a $20,000 owner salary, or

4. The full earning potential of the business is not being realized by the present owner.

In any case, the business, as it is now constituted, is worth something less than the appraised asset value of $100,000. If the profit picture cannot be improved, it will not meet the prospective buyer's return on investment and salary requirements. This points out one of the advantages of this method. It requires the potential buyer to examine profitability, return on investment, and salary, independently.

In some purchase situations, it may be useful to consider one other figure. It's the liquidation value of assets, and it represents the amount that the assets of the business would bring were it to be terminated. This is usually the rock-bottom price for which a business can be purchased. But many businesses that are in a loss situation or where the owner is anxious to sell can be had for something around the liquidation value. Knowing what this figure is for a particular business may help in price negotiations.

FINANCING

Although financing the purchase of an ongoing business may appear to be somewhat beyond the scope of this chapter, a very common form of small business financing can affect the selection process. In theory, there are many alternative methods for a buyer to finance the purchase of a small business. These methods fall into two categories. The first basic category of financing is called equity financing and it includes such approaches as use of the personal friends of the buyer, taking on a partner (and using his or her personal funds), or issuing stock.

The other method of financing is called debt or credit financing. Possible sources of credit include commercial lending institutions, cash value of life insurance, business associates, personal friends, relatives, and the seller.

Despite this apparently long list of sources of funds, in practice it is quite difficult for many potential buyers to raise sufficient money to buy the business they want. Personal friends are limited; many buyers are unwilling to take on a partner; stock is difficult, if not impossible, to sell; lending institutions typically have stringent collateral requirements; cash value of insurance is usually insufficient; and personal loans are often not possible. That leaves only the owner, or seller, as a source of financing. And this is where financing enters the selection process. Some owners are willing to provide financing, and some are not. If your financial position dictates the seller becoming a lender, feel out the seller early on in the evaluation process. See if the possibility exists and to what extent. Obviously, a detailed analysis of the business will do you no good if, in the end, you can't buy it. Quite often, for tax reasons, sellers are willing to finance over 70 percent of the purchase price.

13

ANALYZING
A START-UP
OPPORTUNITY

Small opportunities are often the
beginning of great enterprises.
DEMOSTHENES

The last chapter was devoted to the approach used to selecting a specific ongoing business. Obviously, another approach to entering any business field is to start from scratch. Both methods of getting involved in a small business have unique advantages. Purchase of an ongoing business provides an established sales level, regular customers, and probably most importantly, a track record on which to make a judgment. But starting from scratch also has its attractive features. In many instances, it's the lowest-cost approach to getting into business. This is especially true if the particular type of business lends itself to a small-scale, spare-time start-up. Another advantage of starting from scratch is that it provides more freedom of choice in the particulars of the business. For example, the person who starts from scratch can choose the name of the business, its location, its employees, all the equipment and furnishings. One can, in fact, define its entire personality. There is also a very personal advantage in starting from scratch that's important to many people. And rightly so. It's the pride and self-satisfaction in knowing that you did this all yourself; you started this business from the ground up.

There is no right way of getting into business. Buying an ongoing business is right for some people in some situations. Starting from scratch is right for other people in other situations. You'll have to make this decision yourself. If you're undecided, it might be best initially to keep both options open. This is easy because, as you'll see, a major portion of analyzing a start-up opportunity is finding out about existing (ongoing) competition.

THE TWO DIFFERENT START-UP SITUATIONS

Start-up situations fall into two categories. The first involves starting a business that is very similar to other businesses that are already established. Probably most start-up opportunities fall into this category. Examples include antique shops, most restaurants, shoe stores, machine shops, trucking companies, and so on. The second category of start-up situations is much more difficult to define. Basically it involves starting from scratch a business that is unique, either in the product it makes, the service it provides, or in its approach to doing business. Familiar examples of unique products include the hula hoop and the Pet Rock. The recent trend to car repairs and tune-ups "in the owner's driveway" exemplifies a new service concept. And a unique way of doing business would be something such as competitively priced "telephone shopping and home delivery" of grocery products.

The reason it's important to distinguish between these two different start-up categories is because each has its own market analysis process, as you'll see in next sections of this chapter.

MARKET ANALYSIS OF A "SIMILAR TO" START-UP SITUATION

Not surprisingly, the market analysis of a start-up situation that is similar to other businesses that are already established is much like the market analysis used for already established (or ongoing) businesses. Since market analysis of ongoing businesses was the subject of the last chapter, if you skipped or skimmed that chapter because you knew you were specifically interested in start-up situations only, then you've got some more reading to do; go back and read the last chapter.

Now that you're up on the approach used to select an ongoing business, you're ready to appreciate the subtle, yet sometimes significant, differences in approaches used for analyzing a "similar to" start-up situation.

Probably the best way to describe the analysis approach for a "similar to" start-up situation is by example. And some form of retailing is probably the most appropriate example, because it's the kind of business that is started from scratch more frequently than any other.

Let's suppose that you went through the business type selection process presented earlier in this book and decided you wanted to own and operate a hobby shop that specializes in good-quality model trains and airplanes. At first, you're open to the possibility of either buying an ongoing hobby shop or starting from scratch, so you visit with the owners of several hobby shops that have been offered for sale. But somehow none of them excite you. The neighborhood just wasn't what you'd like in one case, and another shop specialized in arts and crafts. Based on this exposure and the knowledge that there aren't that many hobby shops around, especially that specialize in trains and airplanes, you decide to start a hobby shop from scratch.

But where to begin? Do you look for a storefront first? Or do you start contacting model train and airplane suppliers to find out how much merchandise is going to cost you? Well, you do the same thing you do for any small business analysis. You set up a work plan and a time schedule. Let's go through each major step.

Master List of Questions. Right here in the first step there is an important distinction to be made between selecting an ongoing business and analyzing a start-up situation. The distinction is that questions needed to learn about "starting up" are different than the questions that normally would be on an "ongoing" master list of questions, because the questions should be directed at what you need to know to start and successfully operate the business, rather than on the strengths and weaknesses of a particular ongoing business. The master list of questions for the model train and plane hobby shop should include:

- What are the important considerations in site selection? Teen-age population? Family income level? Accessible and highly visible location? Traffic count? Nearest competitor?

- Are most customers local? Or do many come across town or even many miles because of their special interests? How much do they typically spend on each visit?

- How many square feet of store space are necessary? How is this space divided among display area, storeroom, office, teaching area?

- What kind of lease terms are typical? Flat-rate or percentage payments? How much should rent run per month?

- What kinds and sizes of equipment and display fixtures are needed? How much will these cost? Are used items available? If so, are they desirable?

- What lines of merchandise should be stocked? How much of each? How much opening inventory is needed, and at what cost? What lines are available from suppliers? For what items is future dating possible? What about volume discounts?

- How much money will be required to get started? For rent, fixtures, and equipment? Inventory? Salaries? Contingencies? When should I expect to break even?

- What store hours are typical? Do they vary for in-town or shopping-center locations? Must the store be open on Sundays?

- How is merchandise priced? What kinds of mark-ups are put on each type of product? What should the target be for overall store average markup?

- What is the seasonality of the business? How important is the pre-Christmas selling season? When must orders be placed for Christmas selling?

- How many employees are needed? Should teen-agers or semiretired people be sought out for part-time help? What is the going wage rate? How much knowledge of the product is required?

- What are the most effective approaches to advertising and promotion? What kind of outside sign is needed? What will it cost? Is newspaper advertising worthwhile? Should products or the store image be advertised? Does price advertising generate profitable traffic? Is advertising space in the yellow pages a good approach? What size ad is necessary?

- Is a model-railroader or radio-controlled-airplane club a good promotion tool? Can these types of activities generate profitable revenue or do they only have promotional value?

- What kind of specific financial records should be kept? How are Social Security and withholding-tax obligations handled? What about income-tax considerations? Are most shops incorporated? Why or why not? What are the advantages and disadvantages in this particular form of retailing? How much does incorporation cost and what are the requirements of an ongoing corporation? Did the incorporated owners elect to file income tax under the Subchapter S income-tax provision?

- What licenses and permits are required? How does one go about getting them? How much do they cost?

- What kind of insurance is appropriate? Fire? Liability? Burglary? Auto? Worker's compensation? Fidelity bond? Business interruption? Key person? Employee health? How much will it cost?

- What kind of grand-opening celebration is most effective? Should flyers or a mailing or newspaper advertising be used? How long should the opening last? What specials should be offered?

- How have established stores obtained start-up financing? What is the best way to go about securing financing? What profit and expense estimates and collateral are usually necessary? What are the going interest rates and repayment terms?

It's a long list, isn't it? But there's not a question on the list that's not important. The next step is to develop a list of sources that can provide the answers.

Sources of Information. The "above, below, and beside" approach presented in the last chapter for identifying the right people to talk to is also of value in a start-from-scratch analysis. The three big sources of information for any start-up situation can be identified by answering these questions: Who are the key suppliers to the business (above)? Who are the major customers (below)? Who are the prominent competitors or similar businesses in other market areas (beside)?

Other worthwhile sources include our old standbys: the chamber of commerce, the Better Business Bureau, trade associations, and publications.

In the model-train and airplane hobby shop example, as is the case in most retail situations, the different types of sources are limited. Identification of competitors and similar businesses is easy. But the question "Who are the major customers?" creates a logistics problem. The customers of most hobby shops are very diverse and fragmented. Possibly the membership list of some model-railroading or airplane club could be used to identify some specialized customers. These customers could be useful in pinpointing dissatisfactions with existing hobby shops, additional products, or services that could be offered. But on a priority ranking, customer interviews in most retail start-up situations are way down on the list of usefulness. Customers just can't relate to most of the important questions that need answering.

Identification of the key suppliers (the "above" group) is easy. Some names such as Lionel, Tyco, and Cox are almost household words, and other suppliers' names can be gathered by just browsing in a few stores. But the question arises: Do hobby shops buy direct from these big-name suppliers? Or do they buy from wholesalers or manufacturers' agents? Personally, I don't know the answer. But a person who talks to one or two hobby shop owners will soon find out. Or you can look in a major metropolitan yellow pages, as I just did. It looks as though there are specialized distributors of hobby and craft products, so sales managers at some of these distributors would be the useful contacts.

As far as the right people to talk to, our friend who is starting a hobby shop has just two basic sources of information, hobby shop owners and distributors of hobby products. The third category, customers, will probably be of little value. In fact, the distributors are probably not going to be that great. So that leaves hobby shop owners. Fortunately, hobby shop owners can provide answers to all the important questions.

Because so many of these important questions in a start-up situation relate to "getting started," it's important to talk to at least a few business owners who have start-up experience. Ideally, these owners should have started, in the recent past, a business just like the one being contemplated—but not so recently that they haven't had time to establish a successful operation. Talking to several owners who started two or three years ago will assure that things are pretty much the same now as they were when these people got started. Asking start-up type questions to owners who started their businesses ten or fifteen years ago wouldn't be very productive.

It's important to find owners with recent start-up experience. It would be worth it to drive three or four hundred miles to spend an hour or two with such a person. But there is an alternative, if owners with recent start-up experience in the exact same busi-

ness type cannot be located, then find people who have recently
started a similar, but not the same, type of business. In the hobby
shop example, people who have recently started craft shops or
toy stores would be helpful. The local chamber of commerce or
Jaycees may be helpful in locating these business owners for you.

Completing the Analysis.   The remainder of the market analysis of
a "similar to" start-up situation follows the same form as any
market analysis. The next step is to prepare the questionnaires.
One usually should be made for sources "above", sources "below," and sources "beside." However, in the hobby shop example, since there is only one key source of information—the business owner—one questionnaire will suffice.

The number of interviews necessary to complete the fieldwork
phase of the analysis depends entirely on the particular start-up
situation. Probably six to eight owners and three to four distributors would be sufficient in the hobby shop example. The key
is to do as many as necessary to become comfortable with the
answers to all the important questions. When the fieldwork is
done, you should feel ready to start the business, perhaps not
totally confident of success, but ready to give it a good try.

The final item in the market analysis is the site-selection work.
And this is really one of the first steps in getting started. Details
of the site-selection analysis are included in Chapter 10.

MARKET ANALYSIS OF A UNIQUE
START-UP SITUATION

The market analysis of a unique start-up situation, that is, starting from scratch a business unlike any in existence presents some
difficult problems. The first, and most obvious, is that there is no
track record to ask questions about and learn from. There are no
suppliers, no customers, and no competitors to interview. Yet,
somehow, one would like to develop confidence in the success of
the venture before investing a lot of time and thousands of dollars in it. This suggests some form of test market where a small
sampling of the product is sold through limited outlets to determine customers' acceptance.

But test marketing is not always appropriate. What if the product is too expensive to commit money for even a few market test samples? Or what if the product isn't a product at all, but a service? Then what is to be done?

And then there's one other major problem: how to protect the proprietary nature of the product or service, if some form of test marketing is undertaken. Test marketing will disclose the most closely guarded secret. The retailer and every customer who comes into the store will see the product. Will they try to steal the concept right from under your nose?

Let's deal with the proprietary nature or secrecy issue first. Then several specific market analysis approaches will be described which will help overcome some of the other problem areas.

Secrecy and Confidentiality. The protection of new-product concepts and ideas is a legitimate concern of small business owners, especially if the initial success of the business depends on that single concept. As we all know, there are established legal procedures that afford protection in certain instances. Products can be patented, although it is not an inexpensive process. The SBA has a free publication entitled "Knowing Your Patenting Procedure" (Management Aid No. 49) that will provide some helpful insight. A lawyer's assistance is recommended in preparing and filing patent applications. Brand-name, trademark, and printed-material protection is also available. The U.S. Copyright Office in Washington has a list of publications that can be ordered and which are very informative. The list is entitled "Publications of the Copyright Office."

Some products, by their very nature, are self-protections. Secret-formula food products are a prime example. The flavor recipe for Coca-Cola is such a closely guarded secret that I sometimes wonder if anybody at Coca-Cola knows it. And there is an English muffin company in Chicago that has hundreds of employees, but only two or three know the "secret formula." Another class of products are those protected by their sheer size or complexity. Sometimes a product is so complex or so large that only one or two companies can afford to tool up to produce it.

Unfortunately, there are also products and ideas (especially ideas) that fall into none of the above categories. They cannot be patented or copyrighted and they are not self-protecting. Then what to do? You must be careful and cautious. But do guard against being overprotective. I guess it's like raising children; seek the middle ground. Protect them from danger, but don't be so protective that they are prevented from reaching their full potential.

I'm reminded of a case of what I consider protection to the point of smothering a good idea. Back in 1970, I worked with a young man in a consulting firm in Chicago. Unknown to anyone, including his mother (and properly so in this case), this fellow, let's call him Bill, was writing a book. The book was a guide to "living together." This was long before living together was talked about, let alone considered fashionable. It seems he and his wife lived together, without the knowledge of either set of parents, for a year before they were married. At that time, Bill thought a book on this subject would be a sure best seller. He was also very fearful of someone, anyone, stealing his idea and beating him to market. He was especially fearful of publishers—so much so, in fact, that he didn't dare show any of them the manuscript.

Bill felt he had no choice but to publish and market the book himself, which is just what he did. Composition and printing of 2000 hardbound copies cost Bill over $5000. But that, as it turned out, was the easy hurdle. Successfully marketing the book proved to be impossible. Book distributors and bookstores just didn't want to bother with "small potatoes." Bill just didn't have the clout to get distribution. The timeliness of his topic was demonstrated by the fact that he and his wife did appear on a major Chicago TV talk show and the Chicago *Tribune* did a feature article about the book. But his free promotion was to no avail, because the books just weren't in the stores.

Bill now realizes that he overdid the secrecy bit, because there is very little piracy in the publishing business. And the same thing is probably true in most businesses, for several reasons. First and foremost, I believe that most people are basically honest. But there are some very practical reasons too. The pride of authorship prevents most people from objectively evaluating other people's ideas. It seems to be human nature that only the person who conceives an idea has faith in its success. I, for one, could never have been convinced the CB radios or "uniform potato chips stacked in a tennis-ball can" would be smashing successes. But they are. Another practical reason why piracy is not rampant is the pressure of time. Most people are just so busy doing what they have to do that they don't have time to steal other people's ideas. For example, retailers that are used to test-marketing a product for you probably don't want, or have time, to get into manufacturing. But if your product test goes well, they would sure like to sell a bundle of them for you!

Smothering a product concept can do more harm than good. Don't make that mistake. Who knows, Bill's book may have been a best seller and a major motion picture had he just offered it to the right publisher.

The Market Analysis. The market analysis for a unique product or concept has two separate and distinct purposes. The initial purpose is to evaluate the merits of the product or concept itself. If this evaluation proves out, then the analysis should be extended to determine the best way to start up the business entity that will be an integral part of bringing the idea to market.

Let's look at the approaches that are useful in determining the merits of the product or concept. You're already familiar with the small-scale test-market method. It is described on pages 128 thru 130. This is the best approach to use for smaller retail products that can be manufactured in a batch quantity at an affordable cost.

A modification of this method is to show or demonstrate the product to potential customers to get their reaction. The consulting firm I'm with did this once for a manufacturer of disposable dinnerware. Our client had developed a new concept in disposable plates and cups targeted at the patient food-service market in hospitals. We tested the concept by carrying a suitcase full of various sizes and colors of cups and plates to hospitals all over the country. Food-service managers at these hospitals got a chance to look at and touch the product and also to hear a description of its merits and price competitiveness. This is a good approach to use with some nonconsumer products. When using this approach it's essential to probe for the potential customer's true reaction. The last thing you want to hear is "kind words" that are being dished out just so your feelings won't be hurt. Always ask whether or not the interviewee would actually buy the product. Then dig for the reasons behind the answer.

But what about products where the cost of manufacturing even a few is prohibitively expensive. And what about concepts that are services rather than products. These are two of the "problem" areas I mentioned in the beginning of this section. Fortunately, there is a fairly reliable approach for even these cases. It involves describing the product or service to potential customers to gain their reaction and determine their interest in purchase. Let me illustrate with another example from my consulting experience. Almost all the transmissions used in heavy semitrailer trucks require manual shifting. Several years ago a client came to us with a request to determine the sales potential of an automatic transmission they were developing. Test marketing or even demonstrating the transmission was prohibitive because each prototype unit would cost well over $100,000. It was decided to evaluate this new product by visiting truck manufacturers and major users of trucks. During each visit, the automatic transmission features (size, weight, number of forward gears, estimated price, etc.) would be discussed. It didn't take long after the visits began to reach a conclusion about the sales potential of the product. It was zero or close to it! There was almost universal agreement that a proposed transmission was too long, too high, too heavy, too expensive, and likely to be plagued with maintenance problems! A few weeks of market analysis effort saved this company from developing a very costly lemon. More important to us, this example demonstrates the merits of talking to potential customers about a new product or service concept, even if it can't be shown or demonstrated.

Positive results in evaluating the merits of a product or service suggest that the second phase of the analysis should be carried out. You'll recall that this second stage is where the best approach to bringing the concept to market is determined. Basically this involves getting answers to all the important start-up type questions—questions similar to the ones sited in the hobby shop example. I can hear you say now, "But the hobby shop example was a *'similar to'* start-up situation." We're now talking about a *unique* start-up situation." That's right. But many of the questions are the same. After all, a lease is a lease, financing is financing, and advertising is advertising. These important factors don't change. In this phase of the market analysis, you want to find out all you can about such relevant topics as:

- Key site-selection factors
- Lease consideration
- Building size and facility requirements
- Equipment and fixture needs
- Manufacturing processes
- Financing
- Advertising and promotion
- Personnel
- Pricing
- Seasonality
- Licenses and regulations
- Existing products or services that your new concept is intended to displace or compete with

Where to get these answers? That might require some digging. If the concept is truly unique, then by definition there are no competitors, no "similar to" businesses (and, as noted earlier, potential customers are of little value for start-up type questions). Fortunately, there are businesses that are similar enough to be useful. For example, if the unique product was the hula hoop, then surely toy manufacturers could be helpful in answering advertising, promotion, pricing, and seasonality question. Plastic-product manufacturers could help with facilities, equipment, and processing questions. If you find yourself in the situation of needing answers to start-up type questions for a unique product or service, dig around for people and businesses that have experience that would be of use to you. It may require talking to two or three different types of sources to fit all the pieces of the puzzle together. One group of sources may be helpful for advertising and promotion questions, another group may be able to answer your manufacturing questions, and a third group may be needed for financing and start-up cost information. It will require a lot of work on your part, but the results will be worth it.

14

GETTING OUT AND TALKING TO PEOPLE

*I attribute the little I know to my not having been
ashamed to ask for information, and to my rule of
conversing with all descriptions of men on those topics
that form their own peculiar professions and pursuits.*

JOHN LOCKE

This is going to be the shortest chapter in this book, and yet in many ways it contains the most important message. This chapter has a singular purpose—to emphasize the extreme importance of getting out and talking to people.

You no doubt have noticed that there is a consistent element running through all of the market analysis situations and examples described in the last five chapters. This consistent element is an organized and systematic approach to information gathering. The gathering is done, in the main, through discussions with people who've got the facts and opinions needed to make an informed decision.

In the first chapter of this section, on the approach used by giant corporations, I described a somewhat bizarre incident where I interviewed a secretive inventor as he drove me through the streets for an hour and a half. Then in the next chapter the small business selection process is described in detail, and emphasis is put on the techniques and approaches that are useful in personal and telephone interviewing. The next chapter concentrates on the franchise selection process. There, the importance of probing discussions with franchising company personnel and with franchisees is emphasized. Selecting an independently owned, ongoing business is the topic of Chapter 12. Here it was made clear that the essence of this type of market analysis is to identify the right people and then to ask them the right questions. Basically, you want to know everything that they know about the market and the seller's company that is relevant to the purchase decision. You don't need to know any more, and you can't afford to know any less. And in the last chapter, the trade-offs between protecting a proprietary idea and disclosing, through discussions, some aspects of the concept to get a market reaction are explored. In each of the very different situations covered in these chapters, one key element comes through: getting out and talking to people!

It might not be necessary for me to write this chapter for some people, but there are many others that will hesitate and stop when it comes time to actually get out and meet people face-to-face. It's difficult for some to be sure of their ability to ask probing questions to people they've never even met before. I can sympathize with you if you're in this "not so sure" category. I was there once myself, and I know how it feels.

I'll never forget how hard it was for me to do my first interviews after I joined a management consulting firm. My first assignment was a market analysis of the wood and plastic finishes used on kitchen cabinets. The fellow who was directing the study had "suggested" that I start the fieldwork with a two-day trip to Cincinnati. I was to interview the Formica Corporation and five or six kitchen-cabinet dealers. I was petrified! Why would anyone at Formica see me. What do I know about kitchen cabinets, except that's where the dishes and pots and pans are kept. And why should a dealer—for that matter, five or six dealers—take themselves away from customers and possible *sales* in order to answer my dumb questions. I got my "traveling instructions" on Friday. That weekend I told my wife that I'd probably be going to Cincinnati on Tuesday and Wednesday. That way I'd have Monday to telephone Cincinnati to make appointments. Monday morning came all too soon. During the ride in on the train, I was sure I could do it but when I sat down at my desk, nothing happened. That's wrong, something did happen. I began making up excuses why I couldn't make those calls. First, I didn't know the phone numbers. So I had to get the Cincinnati phone book in the library. Now I had the numbers, but I decided that it was too early to call someone, to call anyone on a Monday morning. So I got a second cup of coffee. Then I spent one hour and a half "researching" some three-year-old government construction statistics. (Somehow I hoped that these reams of data would give me confidence by making me an instant expert. They didn't.) By the time I finished researching, it was almost 11:00 A.M. "That's 12:00 in Cincinnati. Lunch time. No one will be there. I'll have to wait to call until this afternoon." My first call that afternoon was made at 3:00. It wasn't to Cincinnati; it was to my wife: "Carol, I got a little behind schedule. I probably won't be going to Cincinnati until Wednesday."

Tuesday came and went, and I still hadn't picked up the phone. Then Wednesday morning came and went. I was desperate. Luckily my boss was out of town and wouldn't be back until the following Monday, but I had to do something. All I had left was three hours to arrange my schedule. Then I'd spend Thursday and Friday in Cincinnati. It was either make those calls and go to Cincinnati or lose my job.

I dialed a number and heard, "Good afternoon, Formica Corporation." My rehearsed and re-rehearsed opening line escaped me. I had no choice—I hung up the phone. After a slow trip to the men's room I decided I'd better write down my script. Then I phoned again. "Good afternoon, Formica Corporation." I read my line, "Uh, yes, I'm trying to locate your market research manager." Luckily she knew his name. His extension was ringing. It was too late to hang up this time. "Harry Keller here." Remembering my boss's advice to be informal, I blurted out, "Harry, my name is Ken Albert and I'd like to see you tomorrow morning." Thank God Harry was a nice guy. After asking why I wanted to see him, he agreed to a meeting at 9:00 A.M. on Thursday. I was rolling! It took me two and a half work days to make one phone call, but I felt great.

As the comedians say, to make a long story short, I saw Harry and three dealers on my trip to Cincinnati. I even got some good information. Though I didn't do as well as I should have (I forgot to ask some key questions and I was short two dealer interviews), my boss was satisfied with my first attempt, and so was I. I had taken the first step in overcoming my apprehension. I had actually called up and visited living, breathing people. Each time after that, the phone calls and interviews became a little easier, until I was doing it as though I was born to do it.

The most important thing that I learned from this experience is that people, by and large, are friendly and helpful. I found out that people do agree to visit with a complete stranger if they receive a sincere and honest request on the telephone. And I learned that most people really try their best to answer most of the questions asked during a visit. You'll discover these same things, if you'll just give it a try. Maybe you won't be as lucky as I was in getting a yes on the first phone call, but if you hang in there and keep trying, I guarantee that you'll get a lot more yeses than noes. And once you start visiting people you'll start getting answers to your questions, and these answers will lead you to the small business opportunity that's right for you. So don't hesitate, get out and talk to people.

PART
IV
NOW YOU'RE
READY TO BEGIN

CHAPTER

15

SOME HELPFUL HINTS
ON GETTING STARTED

The journey of a thousand miles starts with a single step.
CHINESE PROVERB

When you've completed the business selection process described in the previous two sections of this book, you'll already be off to an excellent start in establishing your own business. This is true because you'll know that you've selected a business opportunity that's right for you and that has a high probability of success. What's more, by going through the selection process, you'll have the added benefit of learning a lot about the business you're about to enter. In fact, it's quite possible you'll have arrived at some conclusions and developed some ideas that will give you a decided advantage over your competition.

As you probably know by now, there are dozens of factors to consider in the actual start-up process of a small business. And this is true whether it's a franchise, an ongoing business, or a start-from-scratch situation. The purpose of this chapter is to highlight some of the most critical getting-started factors and to mention some less conspicious ones that are often overlooked. But please, for your sake, don't stop reading about starting and managing a small business after you've finished this chapter. There are volumes written on this subject, and many are very worthwhile.

START-UP SCHEDULE

One of the first things you should do after choosing a specific business opportunity is to develop a comprehensive start-up schedule. The schedule should include all the major items to be accomplished by you during the start-up period, and it should be keyed to the opening or takeover date.

The need for a start-up schedule for a business that is being started from scratch is obvious, but a start-up schedule is also essential in the other two start-up situations—buying a franchise or buying an ongoing business. Let's examine the details of the start-up schedule for each of the three situations.

If you have decided to start your own business from the ground up, a good start-up schedule can help eliminate a lot of the headaches that otherwise would be associated with the early days of operation. During the selection process you will have heard a lot from business owners concerning "what to do" and "what not to do" in starting your business. The start-up schedule gives you the opportunity to implement all this sage advice. Begin work on your schedule by listing all the things that you must accomplish during the start-up period. For instance, your list might include:

- Lease storefront

- Buy display cases

- Have telephone installed

- Purchase sign

- Incorporate

- Develop recordkeeping system

- Prepare business plan

- Select company name

- Arrange grand opening

- Purchase opening inventory

Now arrange your list roughly in order of "first things first." For example, obviously you'll have to decide on the company name before the incorporation can proceed. Then assign a time period to the accomplishment of each item on your list. The time period should include both the starting time (keyed to your opening date) and the estimated time required to accomplish the task. It will now be possible for you to lay out your start-up schedule, as illustrated in Figure 13.

FIGURE 13
START-UP SCHEDULE

To be accomplished	*March*	*April*	*May*	*June*	*July*
Lease	——————				
Business plan	——————				
Company name	———				
Incorporate		——			
Display cases		————————			
Inventory		————————			
Sign			———————		
Recordkeeping				——————	
Grand opening				——————	
Telephone					——

The importance of a comprehensive start-up schedule for a franchise depends greatly on the specific situation. Some well-established franchising companies assume almost total control of the start-up phase. Otherwise, depending on the franchise you buy, you may be responsible for selecting space and arranging a lease, hiring personnel, ordering supplies, arranging the initial grand-opening promotion, and so on. If this is the case in your situation, a start-up schedule will be invaluable.

The start-up schedule for the purchase of an ongoing business should more properly be called a transition schedule, because its purpose is to coordinate the transition with the previous owner. Items to put on your schedule include:

- Becoming familiar with recordkeeping systems
- Meeting employees and learning their responsibilities
- Brief, get-acquainted meetings with key suppliers
- Visits with key customers
- Briefing on production practices
- Orientation on sales and promotional techniques

START-UP COSTS

It's extremely important to accurately estimate the costs associated with business start-up. This is quite easy to do by separating all costs into two categories. The first category includes all costs that will be incurred only once. The second category includes all regular monthly expenses. These are incurred during the start-up period and every month thereafter.

Let's look at the first category, nonrecurring expenses. The most obvious item in this category is the franchise fee, or business purchase price. Other major nonrecurring expenses include fixtures and equipment, decorating and remodeling, opening inventory, and opening advertising and promotion.

But there are also numerous small one-time expenses that should be estimated, because all these miscellaneous expenses can really add up. An acquaintance of mine just started a land-surveying business which he operates out of a spare room in his home. He couldn't get over the $100 deposit required by the telephone company for his business phone. He's lived in the same house for years and always paid his phone bill on time. But the phone-company policy requires a security deposit on all new business-phone installations "because of the risk of bad debt." This is just one small start-up expense that could be overlooked.

Other small miscellaneous start-up expenses to estimate include sales-tax deposits, business licenses, permits, legal and other professional fees, association and organization dues, petty cash, reserve to carry customers' accounts, travel expenses, et cetera. A reserve fund, to cover unforeseen contingencies, should also be set up.

Regular monthly expenses begin when the business begins, which is usually long before the business itself can generate enough revenue to pay them. Most small business owners recommend that a new business owner have enough money set aside to pay monthly expenses for a three-month period. This amount should be placed in a separate bank account and not used for any other purposes. Major monthly expense items include owner's salary, other salaries, loan payments, maintenance, professional fees, and miscellaneous expenses.

The SBA publishes an excellent guide to estimating business start-up costs. It is Small Markets Aid No. 71, entitled, "Checklist for Going into Business." It includes a worksheet that will enable you to estimate both your one-time and monthly start-up expenses. Of course, the usefulness of the estimates will depend on their accuracy. So if you're not sure of some of the entries, such as monthly advertising expense or employee expenses, pick up the telephone and ask someone who knows. Probably the best bet is one of the business owners you've interviewed in the past.

BUSINESS PLAN

Business planning has grown to become a field unto itself. Volumes have been written on it, it's the subject of business school courses, specialists earn a living showing other people how to do it, and most companies have adopted it, at least to some degree. In fact, many large companies have adopted a formal five-year business plan, which is updated every year.

Emphasis placed on planning is not misdirected. Planning is a necessary function of all businesses, large and small. The primary purpose of a business plan is to guide an organization toward meeting its objectives. It keeps the business itself and all of its decision makers headed in a preselected direction.

In addition to this primary function, the business plan can have an additional important function. It can serve as a sales tool for raising funds, either from private investors or from lending institutions. In this role, the business plan takes on a less functional and more promotional tone.

A well-conceived business plan will be an invaluable asset in guiding your new business. During the start-up phase of your business, you should set aside time to develop it, whether or not it will be needed to raise money. The exercise of preparing it is, in itself, a most valuable experience.

A good business plan starts with a simple, concise statement of the purpose of the business. It then describes the products or service to be provided and their features and appeal to the customers. Next, it briefly notes how the products are to be manufactured or purchased.

Another ingredient of a good business plan is an overview of the people in the business. An organization chart is a must, along with capsule résumés of key personnel. Current and future staffing plans should also be included, along with some indication as to whether you plan to expand using full-time permanent employees, part-time college students, or whatever.

Follow this section with a more detailed section directed at market plans. The major customer group should be defined and described. An analysis of your key competitors' strengths and weaknesses and their estimated market share is a must in this section. Also include a market growth forecast and a sales forecast (by product line or service category) for your company. Current-year, next year's, and the following years' sales should be forecasted. The last important element in the market section is an analysis of marketing strategy. It should describe, in detail, how you expect to accomplish the sales forecast. Promotional plans, advertising budgets, sales staffing, product distribution, and pricing strategies are all key topics.

This marketing section, along with the financial section that follows it, are the heart of the business plan. The financial section should include a forecast of income and expenses and a forecasted balance sheet. A cash-flow statement, which defines the sources and uses of funds, completes the essential financial input.

The next to last major item in the business plan deals with physical requirements. Current and future floor space and major capital equipment requirements should be projected. Considerations should be given to such apparently mundane items as storage and parking space (for customers and employees).

Finally, the business plan should have a section devoted to the future, five or even ten years ahead. It should deal with product concepts, long-range marketing plans, expansion into new territories, possible computerization of bookkeeping, and any other relevant, long-term considerations.

I'd recommend you read several of the books devoted to small business planning. Discuss the subject whenever you can with fellow business managers, to gather further insight. In this way, each updated plan will contribute more toward directing your business toward a prosperous future.

SETTING GOALS

In the beginning, your major goal will no doubt be just to survive, and that's an accomplishment in itself. But a business can't be built on survival alone. You'll need specific goals and objectives to guide your business. This process, setting goals and measuring your progress by them, is really a key part of business planning. Properly, it should be included in your business plan, but I've chosen to treat it as a separate topic because it's so essential to getting off to a good start.

Set realistic goals for your new business. Write down what you expect to accomplish in three months, six months, one year, and five years. Then set a reasonable goal, in months, for reaching the break-even point.

Make sure the goals you've chosen are specific enough to be meaningful and measurable. A goal to "increase sales next quarter" is too vague. Instead, it should read "to increase sales by 10 to 15 percent next quarter." Major goals should be broken down into subgoals so that partial accomplishment or failure can be highlighted.

Once your goals are set, the next step is to plan the actions necessary to meet each goal, and always be sure to assign the responsibility for following through on each action to yourself or an employee.

The final step in this goal-setting process completes the circle. It's a periodic review of goals and actions. At these review points, remedial steps can be taken to correct actions that have fallen short, or goals can be revised to reflect changes in priorities, the economy, and so on. The most critical factor associated with good review is timing. Review sessions should be held frequently enough to correct problems before they are out of control or beyond the point of no return.

The goal-action-review cycle is one of the most powerful management tools. Implement it when you start your business, and it will serve you well in the years to come.

PARTNER(S)

One or more business partners can be a blessing or a curse. First, let's look at the advantages of taking on a partner or two. Partners are an obvious source of capital. If you need more money than you have, a partner may be able to contribute to the cause. In a more human vein, a partner can contribute a great deal to an enterprise by complementing your capabilities. You may lack an outgoing "sales" personality, needed production experience, or business contacts. Another person may be able to bring some of these elements to the business. A third asset brought by partners is moral support. This may not seem like much of an advantage, but it could ultimately make or break a fledgling business. The moral-support factor seems to be especially important in businesses requiring large measures of personal selling. In these situations, the partner who's on a "hot streak" can sustain and encourage the other partners who are in long dry spells, whereas a person trying to go it alone may become discouraged and give up because of poor sales performance.

Having a partner or partners, as I said earlier, also has its drawbacks. The most obvious drawback and maybe the most critical is that the income of the business will be divided. The other major disadvantage of a partnership arrangement is the people problem. If harmony between the partners is lacking, the business will ultimately suffer. Decision by committee and backstabbing have destroyed some very promising businesses.

This brings us to the all-important issue of how to choose a partner or partners. Unfortunately, there is no formula. The best partnerships are probably those that evolve naturally from a business situation, for example. Maybe two disgruntled employees decide to strike off on their own. Or an inventor and a sales representative, who've been lodge brothers for years, form a partnership to exploit a new idea. But if a natural association is not possible, and you feel the need for a partner, nothing says you can't go looking. Good places to search include fellow employees, friends, and competitors' employees.

In some instances, the risk of forming a partnership can be minimized by maintaining control yourself. There's no law saying that a partnership has to have equal stock ownership. You can own 75 percent and your partner 25 percent. In a three-way partnership, two partners can each control 40 percent of the stock and the other the remaining 20 percent. I personally know of a very successful partnership with just this arrangement. Most of the key decisions are made by the two majority partners—who fortunately agree on most everything. The third partner, who isn't always so agreeable, has no choice but to go along.

INCORPORATION

There are three basic legal forms of organization. The first, called a sole proprietorship, is easiest to initiate, and it's relatively free of government regulation. But these two major advantages of a sole proprietorship are counterbalanced by an ominous disadvantage. That is, the owner is personally liable for all claims against the business, which means that not only are the assets of the business vulnerable to loss, but so is all the owner's personal property.

The second basic form of legal organization, the general partnership, is basically a shared, sole proprietorship. It's almost as easy to set up, for it requires no official registration. Each partner is taxed on his or her share of the partnership income, at his or her personal income-tax rate, just as for a sole proprietorship. Again, the ominous disadvantage still lurks in the corner; partnership liability extends to the personal assets of the general partners.

A modified version of the general partnership, called the limited partnership, permits investors to become partners without assuming unlimited liability. Limited partners usually only risk as much as they invest. A limited partnership, however, must have at least one general partner, who, of course, has unlimited liability.

The third basic form of legal organization is the corporation. The corporation is a separate legal entity; it is apart from its owners. Therefore, it can make contracts, it is liable, and it pays its own taxes. Generally, corporation stockholders are not liable for leans against the corporation beyond the amount of their individual investment. This means that if you incorporate your new business, your personal assets are protected from claims against the corporation.

But the corporate form of organization does have its disadvantages. Namely, incorporation is costly (from $1000 to $3000, generally), extensive recordkeeping is necessary, and corporate taxation is heavy (48 percent of net income over $25,000 goes to Uncle Sam). Also, corporate income is subject to a double tax since it is taxed when earned by the corporation and, again, if payed as dividend income to the stockholders.

Fortunately, the federal government has seen fit to allow the small business owner to enjoy the limited liability of the corporate form while escaping its heavy tax burden. It's called the Subchapter S corporation. The Internal Revenue Code permits a closely held corporation (one with up to ten shareholders) to avoid corporate taxation by having each shareholder report his or her share of the corporate income on their individual tax return. This Subchapter S status can be appealing, especially to lower-income, small businesses.

Personally, I would recommend that anyone starting a business should seriously consider the corporate form—with or without electing Subchapter S. It's more costly to form and more cumbersome to live with than the other forms, but in the long run it may be the best bet. Your attorney will be able to present the pros and cons of incorporation and offer a recommendation pertinent to your particular situation.

PROFESSIONAL SERVICES

Unfortunately, it's impossible to avoid the expense associated with professional services, because the intangible products they provide are indispensable in starting and operating a business.

The most famous purveyor of professional services is the lawyer. As mentioned earlier, this professional advice and counsel will be helpful in choosing the form or organization for your business. Once a decision is made, your lawyer can draw up partnership or incorporation agreements. If you're buying an ongoing business, a qualified lawyer can offer invaluable advice on the purchase agreement and can also assist in negotiations. Legal assistance may also be valuable in reviewing contracts with suppliers and customers and in evaluating lease terms. And lawyers can make sure papers are filed properly with city, county, and state governments.

The advice of an accountant who is familiar with small business recordkeeping systems should also be solicited for help in setting up a pattern of bookkeeping that is easy for you to follow and that will make it easier (and less expensive) to audit at tax time. Speaking of taxes, this is where an accountant can really provide a valuable service. The accountant's familiarity with the tax law and with accepted business deductions should put you in a position of paying only the amount of tax that the law requires.

A good local bank contact can also contribute to the success of your business. This is true whether or not you'll require bank assistance for initial capital. Bankers are helpful in establishing separate business accounts and may also be able to offer you billing services and credit systems. If not now, some day you'll probably want to borrow money from your local bank, so you might as well cultivate the banker's friendship from the beginning.

Although less conspicuous than lawyers, accountants, and bankers, the insurance broker provides essential professional services. When you resign your job, you'll be giving up more than a regular paycheck. You'll probably be giving up your health insurance, a life insurance policy, and disability insurance. These will have to be replaced for both you and your family's protection. In addition, your insurance broker can offer a package of insurance coverage to meet your business needs.

Business insurance is discussed in the next section. But before moving on, I'd like to touch on one other type of professional service. There are advertising agencies that specialize in small business accounts, and these agencies can handle your initial advertising program. But many business owners find it less costly to prepare their own ads. During the rush of start-up you may find it convenient to have an agency handle your accounts, then later, if you wish, you can gradually take over the work yourself.

BUSINESS INSURANCE

The key to receiving good legal services is to find and keep a good lawyer. The same logic applies to business insurance, because business insurance is almost as complicated and mind-boggling as the law is. There are a dozen or more different types of business insurance that you should consider. When the time comes for you to make insurance decisions, screen several brokers and carefully compare the coverage they offer. In this section, some of the more important policies are briefly described.

The most common form of fire insurance is extended coverage. It covers the basic loss due to fire and lightning in addition to loss due to windstorm, riot, explosion, hail, and smoke damage. If your business will be in leased quarters, it's a good idea to coordinate your fire insurance with the building owner. Sprinkler insurance is another form of fire-related insurance that you possibly should consider.

Security and theft insurance are probably a necessity. Also included in this category are burglary and safe insurance. In addition to fire and theft, a third major form of property insurance protects against the loss of earnings during an insurable business interruption.

General liability insurance, including both product and company vehicles is also a necessity. Inadequate coverage in this area could ruin a business and threaten the personal assets of a sole proprietorship or general partnership.

Several forms of life insurance are also available. The first, called key man insurance, protects against the loss of a critical employee. In the case of a partnership, it is possible to protect against the repercussions of the death of one of the partners with partnership insurance. Because of the complexities of this type of situation, the services of a lawyer as well as an insurance agent are usually necessary to ensure the continuity of the business and to provide to the deceased partner's beneficiaries an equitable compensation. For the corporate legal structure, a similar coverage is available. It can ensure continuity of control by providing for the repurchase of the stock (by the corporation) of a deceased shareholder. This prevents the heir of the shareholder from intervening in the affairs of the business.

Several different types of bonding may also be relevant to your situation. The fidelity bond placed on an employee reimburses the employer if the employee steals company funds. This type of coverage is appropriate for all employees who have access to company funds. The security bond guarantees satisfactory completion of a prescribed job. General contractors use this form of bond to protect against the failure of subcontractors to complete a job for which they have been hired.

Don't forget medical-surgical insurance for your employees, and you can cover yourself as a part of the group.

FINANCING

In Part III of this book, the possibilities of franchisor financing and seller financing were discussed. However, the most common source of financing to the small business owner is the commercial loan department of local banks. Many of these loans are guaranteed (up to 90 percent) by the SBA. Commercial loans are the subject of this section.

What is needed to get a loan from a commercial bank? First, most institutional lenders require a significant portion of the starting capital be contributed by the business owner (or other investor) from their own funds. In many cases, "a significant portion" means half. So if you have a $60,000 start-up cost, you'll have to come up with at least $30,000 on your own.

If you need start-up financing, it's time to polish up your business plan, which was discussed earlier in the chapter. Lending institutions will require a great deal of specific information as part of the loan application. Much of this information is part of your business plan. A listing of the most common items requested by banks when considering a loan is presented below:

1. A statement of the purpose of the business, including brochures, booklets, and product literature.

2. An explanation of the corporate structure and organization. This section should include a résumé of each major owner, with the general background and business experience of each. Previous experience in the proposed business venture is considered highly desirable. Personal financial statements of each owner are also essential.

3. A well-thought-out explanation of what the money is to be used for, specifically how much is being sought and how it will be repaid.

4. A statement summarizing the future outlook for your business. Include any information you have gathered concerning your competitors' position and also briefly describe your plans for expansion. Your market strategy should also be presented.

5. Projected statement of income and expenses for the next two to four years of operation. Some in-

stitutions require projections for the duration of the loan.

6. A sales forecast in dollars and units. If possible, this should be segregated by product or service category.

7. Proof that the business has adequate property and casualty insurance.

It's always a wise idea to "shop around" for a loan, just as you would do it buying anything else. Don't go to the bank with the subconscious attitude that you know you're not worthy of the loan. Rather, project quiet confidence, not to the point of cockiness, but enough to give the impression that you know what you're doing and you know where you're going.

LAWS AND REGULATIONS

Licenses are required to operate many types of businesses. These licenses are typically granted by state, county, and local governments. Among the business operators subject to licensing regulations are restaurants, beauty shops, contractors, appliance repair, and on and on. The list varies greatly depending on the locale. As is true with most laws and regulations, it's best to check with people who know to determine what licenses are required for your business. Fellow business owners, lawyers, and city officers are some of the people to ask.

You'll probably be concerned with zoning laws and building codes. Zoning laws dictate where specific types of businesses can be located. And building codes control the structure of the place of business itself. If you're planning to start a business in your home, it's especially important to understand the local restrictions and limitations, or else that neighbor whom you could never get along with may shut you down with a phone call to city hall.

There is a whole group of unrelated federal and state laws that you must comply with. These include federal and state consumer protection laws, environmental protection laws, and wage and labor relation laws. National trade associations in the line of business you're entering can be very helpful in guiding and assisting you in these areas. Quite often these trade associations are active lobbying organizations or have worked with the legislature in formulating the laws. A phone call or letter to the appropriate association will get you off to a good start.

If you'll be operating a manufacturing facility, you should also be aware of the provisions of the Occupational Health and Safety Act (OHSA). This act, which pertains to the work environment of employees, has required businesses to reevaluate a good many of their operations and procedures.

Tax laws, at the federal, state, and local level, affect all types of businesses. Because of the magnitude of the impact of all these forms of taxation and because of their complexity, it's very important for you to familiarize yourself with the tax laws. At the federal level there's income tax, Social Security, excise and unemployment taxes. State taxes can include income, unemployment, sales, and franchise tax. And local taxes may include sales, real estate, and personal property among others. There are two publications that are very helpful in explaining the tax laws. The first is the federal "Tax Guide for Small Businesses," Publication 334. The other, published by the SBA is Small Markets Aid No. 142, "Steps in Meeting Your Tax Obligations."

STATIONERY AND OTHER ODDS AND ENDS

By now you no doubt realize that there are a lot of things to do during the start-up of a small business. It's essential to do all the important things. I've tried to share some insight about these, so far in this chapter. But there are many other things that are not really essential or that important but that you should try to get done. I call them odds and ends, and that's what they are. A whole laundry list of things such as stationery, business cards, order forms, keys, coffee machines, et cetera.

There's no way that I can prepare a checklist of these things for you, because every business has a unique group of odds and ends. But I have a suggestion that will help you make your own checklist. Begin by taking a clean sheet of paper, sit down in a quiet place, and think about each aspect of the business. Consider it from every point of view. When you think of something, jot it down. Give special attention to your business as seen by the customer. If you can avoid it, you don't want to forget anything that will leave your first customers with a negative impression.

After you're done thinking, it's time to review all the interview notes you took while selecting your business. It won't take you long; you'll surely find some odds and ends to add to your list.

A final method of adding to the completion of your list is to visit one or two businesses like yours. Take along a small note pad. If it's a retailing type operation you may want to pose as a customer. Linger as long as you can and look for odds and ends.

In the process of developing your odds-and-ends list, you may discover some things that are important enough to add to your business start-up schedule. Act on all the other items as your time and priorities permit.

MINIMIZING YOUR RISK

Risk is an inherent part of any small business venture. You've already gone a long way toward minimizing your risk by selecting the right small business for you. Now that you're about to begin that business, there are some strategies you can follow to lower your risks even further.

The most obvious way to minimize your risk is to start your business on a part-time basis while keeping your job. This approach is well suited to some forms of businesses, of which the mail-order business is a perfect example. I know of many mail-order businesses that were started on a part-time basis. I'm reminded of an article I read about a couple who started selling fruitcake by mail while they were both college students. The business has expanded to the point where it's a full-time career for both of them, and gross sales are about $400,000 a year. Not bad for a part-time start!

I also know of a man who agreed with his wife that he wouldn't quit his job until his very risky "business" netted in one year what he regularly brought home in salary. Eventually it happened. He just recently quit his full-time job with the telephone company to pursue the business of writing plays. It's even possible to hold down a full-time job while starting a retail business that's open sixty-five hours a week. I know of two men who did this very thing. They hired a clerk to run the store on weekdays and then took turns operating it on evenings and Saturdays. So keep this approach in mind and give it a try if it's at all appropriate.

Another way of minimizing risks, which is applicable to more situations, is to start on a small scale, as small a scale as possible. Bigger isn't necessarily better, especially when you're just starting out. Take the restaurant business, for example. One of the most popular and highly rated Italian restaurants in Chicago started as a carry-out pizza stand. Several years after its founding, a few tables were added. Then later, an adjoining dining room and other Italian foods were added. Next came a cocktail lounge. The restaurant today has three large dining rooms, a cocktail lounge, and a jam-packed parking lot.

A third way of minimizing risks is to keep your overhead down, a suggestion applicable to all businesses. By overhead I mean all fixed costs including rent, equipment, number of employees, and amenities such as wall-to-wall shag carpeting, oversize solid-oak desks, and private secretaries. A friend of mine followed this advice to the letter when he started a one-man consulting firm. Instead of renting a downtown office, buying furniture, and hiring a full-time secretary, he put a used desk and bookshelf in his basement, installed a phone, and made arrangements with an outside typist to prepare his correspondence and reports. He knew that plush offices for small consulting firms serve only to satisfy the occupant's ego, since clients very seldom visit a consultant's office. His at-home office is saving him well over $1000 a month, money that otherwise would have been going for nonessentials.

Unnecessary overhead is a continuing danger. It's especially tempting to indulge in it after the first flush of success. Try to resist.

Specific management or work experience in a business like the one you plan to start, in some situations, may also lower your risk. The need for this experience is, of course, a personal judgment. If the business of your choice is totally foreign to your own experience, then maybe some direct work experience is advisable. For example, if you plan to start a men's clothing store, and you feel the need for some direct experience, it may be possible to find a part-time evening sales job in a clothing store.

However, if you have some applicable work experience, or if your business choice is highly structured, you can probably start it without added experience. Highly structured new businesses include almost all franchise situations. In most franchises, the business concept is so well established and the training program so comprehensive that no experience is necessary.

16

A WORD TO
YOUR SPOUSE

*Oh, the comfort, the inexpressible comfort, of feeling
safe with a person, having neither to weigh thoughts nor
measure words, but pouring them all right out, just as
they are, chaff and grain together; certain that a faithful
hand will take and sift them, keep what is worth keeping,
and with the breath of kindness blow the rest away.*

REX COLE

Some people have a tendency to think of the starters of businesses as males and of spouses as female. In fact, if this chapter were written not too many years ago, it probably would have been called "A Word to Your Wife." But even a decade ago that kind of title would have been inaccurate. Many women have been owners of businesses, and the women's movement has increased both the number of women business owners and the number of women who are seriously considering starting their own businesses.

There are many things that spouses of either sex can do to help during the start of a small business. These things, including understanding, patience, encouragement, and participation, are among the topics in this chapter.

UNDERSTANDING YOUR SPOUSE'S MOTIVES

It is difficult for many people, especially spouses, to understand what drives a person to start his or her own business. Why would anyone give up a secure job, risk the savings of a lifetime, work long, hard hours, and do it all with no guarantees of success—especially if there are children and a mortgage involved. Why would anyone do such a seemingly irrational thing.

Well, everyone does it for different combinations of reasons. Surely freedom, self-satisfaction, and fulfillment are important, and so is the desire to escape the many negative aspects of most jobs. Unfortunately, research studies and such best-selling books as Studs Terkel's *Working* have emphasized the dissatisfactions that vast numbers of people find in their jobs. No doubt, your spouse is in this category, or thoughts of self-employment would never have surfaced in the first place.

It's important for you to understand why your spouse wants to start a business. If you don't know, you should find out. In the near future, when you have some quiet time together, bring up the subject. Talk about it. Find out his or her motives, and share your feelings on the subject.

Starting a small business, in many cases, boils down to a difficult choice between the potential risks of the business and the security of being an employee. I'd like to offer my personal opinion on this decision, for what it's worth. If your spouse never gives his or her own business a try, the thought of what might have been may be a haunting one forever. At least, if a person tries and falls short, he or she will know that they had the will and courage to give it their best. And if one tries and succeeds, you will have a happier, more fulfilled spouse to share the rest of your life with.

BE PATIENT

The start-up phase of a business is extremely time-consuming. As you can imagine, there are a multitude of things to do, including dealing with unforeseen emergencies and unexpected problems. On top of all the start-up-related activities, there are the routine necessities of doing business, so it's obvious that your spouse will be putting in a great deal of time in the beginning.

Starting a business also requires intense and almost total concentration. The start-up is the most critical time in the life of a business. At times you may feel that your spouse is married to the business instead of to you. He or she may be working seven days a week for twelve to fourteen hours a day. Your social life will be impossible. Friendships with other couples may suffer because your spouse can't find the time to get together with them.

To make things even worse, quite possibly there may be a shortage of money. I know of a family who went without furniture in the living room and curtains on the windows during the time one member was starting a business.

But take heart. The demands on your spouse's time and energy will eventually begin to ease. It may take six months or it may take several years, but the time will come when your spouse will return to something approaching normal working hours. I know of two people who worked incessantly for almost three years to establish their business. Now they share the managerial responsibility, each working about half time, and each making close to $100,000 a year.

BE SUPPORTIVE AND ENCOURAGING

You may be somewhat put off by a spouse suggesting that you be supportive and encouraging. After all, you say, "I'm always supportive and encouraging. Isn't that what marriage is all about?" Yes, you're right. But the beginning of a new business venture is special. It needs an extra measure of support and encouragement.

An encouraging word can mean a great deal. I still have a card on my desk that my wife gave me one January when I was about to venture out into the world of the self-employed. It read:

> A very Happy Birthday, My Darling. I pray that this
> year will be very special for you. . . . And that I can
> be a help to you. I love you and I believe in you.

This simple message was deeply reassuring to me, at a time when I needed it the most.

Support and encouragement can also be much more direct. It

can even include persuasion. A restaurant owner I know adamantly refused to get a liquor license because he felt it would ruin the family atmosphere of his one-year-old business. He kept saying, "I can't stand drinking." But the business was suffering, and his wife was sure it was because people couldn't get beer or wine to go with pizza, the specialty of the restaurant. At her insistence—and I mean insistence—he gave in and bought the license. Business is good, and as he says, "I realize now that people come here to eat, not to get drunk. I've still got a family atmosphere and now I've got customers to appreciate it."

A spouse's support and encouragement can mean the difference between success and failure of a new business.

MAKE ADJUSTMENTS AT HOME

As I mentioned earlier, the months just preceding and the month just following the start-up of your spouse's business are the most critical and also the most time-consuming. Your spouse will be experiencing a good deal of strain and anxiety and will be extremely busy. It's quite likely that all of this will be at least somewhat disruptive to your homelife. There's probably no way to eliminate all these disruptions, but there are some things you can do to make this period a little easier on everyone involved.

Begin by trying to assume more than your normal share of household duties and responsibilities. If your spouse is starting the business, take over his or her routine chores. Do it without being asked, and it will be appreciated even more.

New businesses have a way of destroying household schedules. Dinners planned for six dry out in the oven at seven-thirty. Evenings and weekend time become totally unpredictable. You'll have no choice but to try to cope as best as you can. Choose meals that can be rewarmed or prepared in a short time. Don't make plans for evenings and weekends without talking them over with your spouse, and then be prepared to change plans at the last moment.

Your children, especially if they're younger, should be forewarned that, for a while Mommy and Daddy is going to be very busy and that the time available for playing and doing things as a family will be severely limited for awhile. If your spouse is operating the business out of your home, or if working at home after hours is part of the routine, your children need to know that "working at home" means that interruptions and disturbances must be minimized. I'd like to share my personal experience in this area with you. I'm writing this book at home during the summer months. My two boys, ages six and eight, are home on summer vacation. Is it possible to write a book under these circumstances? Well, I'm getting near the end, so I guess the answer is yes. And I'm sure I owe it all to my wife. The week before I began, she told the boys that they were to pretend that I wasn't home, that I was at the office, when the study door was closed. The first few days of writing were a little rough. I was interrupted to play baseball, to glue a toy, and to look at a drawing, among other things. But after three or four days, with a lot of urging from my wife, the children shaped up. They even stopped sliding messages under the door! If your spouse is working at home, please try to be as helpful as my wife has been to me.

One last point on making adjustments at home. This is directed to you "nonspouses" (in the context of this chapter, the nonspouses are the ones starting the business). If your spouse is working part- or full-time to help tide things over while you're starting your business, then you should try your best to pitch in on some of the household chores. Straighten the place up once in a while or do the dishes, or even tackle the laundry. The change of pace will take your mind off your business problems for an hour or two.

TAKE AN ACTIVE ROLE

You've probably already given some thought to the idea of helping your spouse in his or her business. If you haven't done so, why don't the two of you discuss the possibilities. Most businesses need somebody to do such things as typing, answering the telephone, and helping with the recordkeeping. I think it's a good idea to have spouses actively participate in the family business. To encourage you, I'd like to share a few specific examples where people not only participated, but also made meaningful contributions to their spouse's business.

A friend of mine has started a part-time business that involves buying inner-city rental property, remodeling it, and reaping the benefits of higher rents and property appreciation. He's been doing this for about four years while maintaining a full-time job that requires large doses of out-of-town travel. This arrangement has been made possible because of his wife's active participation in the business. She screens potential tenants, collects rents, and handles tenant complaints. She also acted as a general contractor for the renovation of an entire building. This responsibility included coordinating, supervising, and reprimanding (when necessary) eight hard-nosed subcontractors!

My second example involves a wife who contributed a great deal to her husband's restaurant business. The business had a modest beginning—a hot-dog stand operating out of a small trailer. In the early days, she brought their two toddlers to the stand each morning. They played in the back of the station wagon as she helped her husband set up for the day's business. She also spent many long hours waiting on customers. When the stand became a sit-down restaurant, she did everything from refinishing fifty old wooden chairs to wallpapering the bathrooms. And even now, when a waitress or cook doesn't show up, she's on emergency call to help out. She does it cheerfully and with the sure knowledge that she and her husband are making it together.

And husbands also make meaningful contributions to a wife's business. I know of a man, an executive who travels a good deal and is married to a small business owner, who often lends a helping hand in his wife's beauty salon. On Saturday mornings, the busiest day of the week, he removes the curlers from the heads of customers waiting to be combed out.

17

BASIC KEYS
TO SUCCESS

*There is only one real failure in
life that is possible, and that is,
not to be true to the best one knows.*

FARRAR

The most critical period in the life of a new business, according to the Dun and Bradstreet *Business Failure Record,* is the second through the fifth year of operation. Their statistics indicate that less than 10 percent of business failures take place during the first twelve months of existence. This says to me that just about any business, no matter how poorly conceived or managed, can survive till its first birthday party. But the next four years are the killers—a whopping 58 percent of business failures, according to Dun and Bradstreet, take place between the age of one and five. After the fifth year, the failure rate drops off dramatically.

There has been a lot said and written about why these failures occur. I guess these autopsies are necessary and informative, but in this chapter I'd like to take the opposite view. I want to emphasize the attributes present in most successful small business ventures, the attributes that help a business make it through the high-failure period during its first five years of existence.

The beauty of these attributes, or basic keys to success, is that they are present in successful businesses, regardless of type or location. They are truly common denominators of success.

DETERMINATION, DESIRE, AND ENTHUSIASM

As all of us who've been employees know, determination, desire, and enthusiasm are rare commodities in the world of the jobholders. It's unusual to find an employee who has the determination to do the best job possible, the desire to do more than is required, and the enthusiasm to really care about the work. Among successful independent business owners, the opposite is true.

Successful small business owners do the best job possible, they do more than the job requires, and they do care. They care a lot. It is hoped that you too will find determination, desire, and enthusiasm—for whatever reason. Some business owners are motivated by money, some by status, some by pride, and others because they have found a cause. The reason behind the motivation doesn't seem to matter. It's the resulting drive that counts.

I'm reminded of a case where desire and enthusiasm won the day. A large truck company had a troubled dealership for sale in Denver. There were two finalists in the bidding. One was a well-heeled truck dealer who lived in Texas. He proposed to purchase the dealership with cash and hire a manager to run it. The other finalist was a team of two men who knew almost nothing about running a truck dealership and who would require headquarters financing in order to make the purchase. As one of these men explained to me, "We were shocked when they chose us over the guy from Texas. Later we found out the decision was based on the hungry look in our eyes." Well, these two "hungry looking guys" proved to be winners. They paid off the financing obligation in three years and have built a very successful dealership. Their determination, desire, and enthusiasm got them a business and helped them make it a success.

KNOW YOUR BUSINESS AND MARKET

You've already learned a great deal about your business and market in the process of making your business selection, but there's always more to know. One of the most interesting aspects of having a business of your own is the opportunity it affords for continual exposure to new people and new ideas. Knowing your business and market by keeping up on what's going on is a basic key to small business success.

Join and take an active part in the activities of local business organizations such as the chamber of commerce and the Jaycees. Business owners in all fields have much in common. Membership in this type of organization will expose you to new opportunities and new approaches to solving business-related problems.

As for the trade association contacts you made earlier, now might be a good time to join the association that is appropriate to your business area. Belonging to a good trade association can provide you with an invaluable source of business knowledge. It will put you in direct contact with a group of business owners who share your interests and problems. (And besides, the annual meetings and conventions are a lot of fun.)

Another way to keep up with your business and market is to read. The *Wall Street Journal* is essential as a starter. You also should subscribe to some of the major business magazines. I've always found *Forbes* and *Business Week* to be extremely informative. Finally, subscribe and read (or at least skim) all the trade publications in your particular field. Many are available at no cost.

Some business owners make the mistake of isolating themselves from equipment and merchandise suppliers. Business owners are especially prone to do this with suppliers with whom they have no active dealings. But all suppliers are great sources of information. They know who's buying what, they know about new processes and new merchandise, and they always know a lot about what's "going on." Suppliers enjoy discussing their knowledge with customers and potential customers, so have lunch with them once in a while. It may be time well spent.

Above all else, keep up with the needs of your customers, especially if you're serving a commercial market. Try to know your customers' business as well as they do. It's important to convey a genuine concern about your customers' problems. They should feel that they can confide in you. It could well be that a customer's problem will become an attractive new product or service opportunity for you.

ADEQUATE CAPITAL

Estimating how much money you'll need to start up your business was a part of the subject matter in Chapter 15. Tips on obtaining financing was also a topic of that chapter. The purpose of this section is to emphasize the extreme importance of adequate capital to the success of any new business. Nothing worse can happen than to run out of money just when your business is beginning to turn the corner.

The first step in guaranteeing adequate capital is to do everything possible to make sure that your estimate of start-up expenses is accurate. The best way to do this is to make your estimates as detailed and comprehensive as possible. However, no matter how much effort you expend in estimating, some degree of uncertainty will still be present. To assure that your capital is adequate, a contingency fund over and above the estimated total start-up cost should be set up. This fund will then be available for unforeseen expenses, and it will be available just in case it takes longer for your business to become self-sustaining than you had thought. An unforeseen downturn in the economy can play havoc with undercapitalized new businesses.

Now that you've done your best to calculate the amount of money you'll need, don't make the mistake of starting with less. If you have difficulty raising the needed money, continue your search for financing. At the same time, put as much as you can in your savings account.

GOOD RECORDKEEPING

Good records are an essential part of operating a successful business, for a number of reasons. Accurate and up-to-date records are necessary to exercise managerial control. This is true because they allow the owner to accurately answer such questions as:

> What was my sales volume last week, last month? How do these figures compare with week-earlier and month-earlier totals? How much do I owe suppliers and other creditors? What is my gross profit margin?

Proper management of a business also requires spotting problem areas early. Responsible records will tell you:

> Who owes me money? What are my losses from credit sales? Who is delinquent? How often do I turn over my inventory? Which items in my inventory are obsolete?

Answering questions like the ones in the two preceding groups and answering cost-related questions provide a business owner with the opportunity to maximize profits. Key cost-related questions include:

> What were my expenses? Am I taking advantage of cash discounts for prompt payment? Have I received all my outstanding credit for returned merchandise? How does my sales expense compare with last year?

Another major reason that good records are an integral part of a good business operation is to satisfy government requirements. For example, payroll records must meet the requirements of Workmen's Compensation, Social Security, wage hour laws, unemployment insurance, and withholding taxes. Accurate overall financial records are necessary to justify your federal and state income-tax returns.

If good management and government reasons aren't enough to justify good recordkeeping, how about three more reasons. First, it is very difficult, if not impossible, to obtain financing without good records. Second, good records are the basis of projecting meaningful budgets for the months ahead. And thirdly, accurate and complete records are needed to substantiate the performance of the business if you decide to sell.

It's important to recognize that the term *recordkeeping* does not apply exclusively to financial records. Financial records are an integral part of a good recordkeeping system, but there are many nonfinancial records that are also important. These include inventory records, purchasing records, credit records, personnel records, production records, engineering change records, and so on.

There are a number of prepackaged recordkeeping systems available. These are designed for use primarily by small businesses. Some are designed for use by many types of businesses, and others are specifically applicable to a particular business, such as barber shops, drugstores, music stores, and service stations. Most of these prepackaged systems are available in stationery stores. It might be worth looking into a sampling of them. For a bibliography of recordkeeping systems, see the SBA's Small Business Bibliography No. 15, "Recordkeeping Systems— Small Stores and Service Trade."

One caution about recordkeeping. There is a danger, in the long run, of overdoing it. Once your record system is established, do not add additional recordkeeping tasks unless you can answer yes to the following questions:

1. Do I really need this information?

2. Can't I get it in a usable form from some existing source?

3. Is the value in having the information worth the extra cost associated with collecting it?

DELIVER VALUE TO YOUR CUSTOMERS

Henry Ford, the man who revolutionized the production of the automobile, is attributed with saying, "The man who will use his skill and constructive imagination to see how *much* he can give for a dollar, instead of how little he can give for a dollar, is bound to succeed." This quotation captures the message of this section.

Value is a difficult commodity to define or to measure; it is very nebulous. But somehow, consumers are able to sense its presence. They know when they are receiving quality and consistency and service. It's a feeling more than anything else, but just the same, to the consumer, it's a most important feeling.

The obvious purpose of delivering value to your customers is to make them feel satisfied with your product or service. If customers aren't satisfied, you've probably lost them forever. But if they are satisfied, they'll continue to buy from you and they'll recommend you to others.

Auto repair centers are notorious for creating unhappy customers. A business owner in Chicago has capitalized very successfully on this discontent. His auto repair business, coyly named Rip-off Auto Repair, offers personal service and reasonable prices. Customers can talk directly to mechanics, the mechanic explains to them what has to be done, and customers are invited to watch the repairs. Rip-off is delivering value to its customers. You should strive to do the same.

PROFITABLE PRICING

There is no escaping it, profit is the name of the game. You have to at least break even, in the long run, and pay yourself a reasonable salary, to stay in business. You can't afford to deliver value to your customers at a loss to you. Don't make the mistake of being so price competitive that you sell yourself right out of business.

A good overall pricing policy makes sure your average price is not too high to build volume or too low to cover expenses and provide a fair return on investment. Of course, competitive pressures and marketing strategies will require you to seek different gross margins for each type of product or service you sell. For example, food stores have an average margin of about 22 percent, but some items are heavily advertised, to build traffic, at a price at or below cost. Other highly competitive products regularly have only a 10 percent margin. To balance things off, many speciality items have gross margins as high as 40 or 50 percent. So products have a great variability in profit contribution, and constant monitoring is required to guarantee that the overall margin goal is being realized.

It's extremely important, especially very early on in a new business, to make sure your margins are sufficient to cover not only obvious expenses but also the great number of hidden costs. Hidden costs include markdowns, shrinkage, spoilage, bad debt, credit charges, and factory and office overhead. This is difficult to accomplish for a new business, because newly created record systems are usually not responsive, or complete enough, to provide the essential cost information. Instead of relying on records, it may be necessary to set individual product margins based on other information. Fellow business owners and suppliers may be able to provide you with typical gross margin figures for specific products.

GOOD MANAGEMENT

Good management is the lifeblood of a successful business. Your competitors will require you to be a good manager, if you are to survive. The study of management should become your lifetime vocation, and there is enough information available on the topic to consume three lifetimes. I remember my first day in a management class in business school. The professor passed out a six-page, single-spaced bibliography of books dealing with management development and organization improvement. And then he said that these were *some* of the good ones to become familiar with.

Obviously, the space devoted to good management in this book has no purpose except to emphasize its importance. Self-initiative will be needed to expand your management skills.

Management functions at three levels in a business organization. The first level is directed at managing the course of the business itself. It involves setting objectives for the business and choosing strategies to meet those objectives. The second level at which management functions is in managing the people who in turn manage others. It is at this level that so much has been written about the importance of delegating authority to the managers. The third and last level of management is directing the work and the people doing it. This level involves organizing the work and supervising its completion.

In most small business situations, at the beginning anyway, the owner is concerned only with the first and third levels of management. This is true only because the organization is too small to require a level of managers between the owner and the workers. However, as business expands, it is essential to develop a management team and to give them the leeway to function responsibly. Earlier, I patted Henry Ford on the back for his astute observation about the wisdom of delivering a full measure of value to customers. Well, it seems that Henry has his shortcomings too. The decline of the Ford Motor Company during the thirties has been attributed by modern business writers to Mr. Ford's refusal to develop a management team. He insisted that his executives function as personal assistants and as extensions of his decision-making authority. This misguided decision, trying to run a large business as a one-man proprietorship, almost ruined the company.

Most management experts agree that good management involves five basic functions. I'm going to very briefly set them out here just to stimulate your thinking. The first function of management is to set objectives, as stated earlier. The second objective is to organize, which entails analysis and classification of work and grouping these into an organizational structure. The third function of management is to communicate with and motivate the people in the organization. This is essential, because it's the people who, in the final analysis, get the job done. How well they do it depends on the quality of communication and the degree of motivation. The fourth function of good management is follow-up, or the measuring of performance and results. Finally, it is the responsibility of good management to develop people, not only in their present jobs, but in anticipation of future advancement.

DON'T HESITATE TO ASK FOR HELP

By now you know that people can be very helpful in assisting in the selection of a small business opportunity. Well, they can be just as helpful during the life of your business. All you've got to do is ask.

The most obvious sources of business advice are your professional service friends. Depending on the problem, your lawyer, accountant, or banker may be able to help, or to steer you to someone who can. Another source of ready help is the professional business healer—the management consultant. Some consultants specialize in the small business area. These people know that you won't have a lot of money to spend, so they won't sock you with a $10,000 or $20,000 proposal. There is a wide variety in the capabilities of individual consultants, so it's always wise to shop three or four before you buy, and always ask for references.

The SBA is also a very valuable source of help. People at the SBA are exposed, on a daily basis, to the problems of small business owners. They can tell you how other business owners went about solving problems similar to yours. The Service Corp of Retired Executives (SCORE), a part of the SBA, can lend years of experience to your small business problem.

A final source of help is your fellow business owners. They may have already lived through and solved the same problem that is now driving you crazy.

APPENDIX

USEFUL INFORMATION
SOURCES

- The Small Business Administration provides extensive consultation services and aids in financing of small businesses. Also valuable:
    Free management assistance publications; *Publication SBA 115A* is a general directory and order form for this series.
    For-sale booklets; *Publication SBA 115B* is a general directory and order form for this series.

- *Small Business Reporter* published at irregular intervals on various topics. Available free at any Bank of America office, or may be ordered from:
    Bank of America
    Dept. 3120, P.O. Box 37000
    San Francisco, CA 94137

- Sources of typical operating ratios for financial analysis:
    Expenses in Retail Business (National Cash Register Company)
    Barometer of Small Business (Accounting Corporation of America)
    Annual Statement Studies (Robert Morris Associates)

- *Tax Guide for Small Businesses,* U.S. Internal Revenue Service, published annually.

- Classified telephone directories

- *Business Publications: Rates and Data,* Standard Rate and Data Services, Inc., Chicago, published monthly. Provides a complete listing of business and technical magazines and periodicals.

- *National Trade and Professional Associations of the U.S. and Canada and Labor Unions,* Columbia Books, Chicago, published annually.

- *Encyclopedia of Associations,* Gale Research Co., Detroit, 1964 to date, biennial, 3 vols. Listing of nonprofit membership organizations in such fields as science, engineering, education, social welfare, health, and medicine.

- *Thomas Register of American Manufacturers,* Thomas Publishing Co., Inc., New York, 1910 to date, annual. Comprehensive 10 volume guide to products, manufacturers and trade names.

- *National Directory of Newsletters and Reporting Sources,* Gale Research Co., Detroit, 1966. A reference guide to national international, and selected foreign newsletters, information services, financial services, association bulletins, training and educational services.

- *The Readers' Guide to Periodical Literature,* The H. W. Wilson Company, New York, 1905 to date. Index of some 180 magazines.

- Low cost market surveys available from organizations such as:
  Predicast, Cleveland, Ohio
  Frost and Sullivan, New York, N.Y.

- Securities and Exchange Commission annual *10-K Reports* and quarterly *10-Q Reports* give valuable information about individual companies, as well as industry-wide analysis.

- Dun and Bradstreet publications provide an accurate guide to credit and other financial informations on various companies.
  Million-Dollar Directory, published annually.
  Individual company reports

- Individual company publications
  Annual reports
  Brochures and product catalogs
  Distribution lists
  Price lists

INDEX